THE AUTHOR

BEN WHITNEY is Education Welfare Specialist Officer for Staffordshire LEA and Associate Lecturer at Bilston Community College. He is a qualified social worker, and has also worked for social services and in the voluntary sector.

He has worked for Staffordshire LEA for eight years and developed a national reputation as a writer and trainer in education welfare issues, especially the Children Act 1989, truancy, exclusions and child protection. He is a member of the National Association of Social Workers in Education and has regularly contributed to regional and national training events, conferences, etc.

His responsibilities include delivering and organising training on attendance and pupil welfare issues for teachers and other colleagues, and the development of policy and procedures for Staffordshire LEA Education Welfare Service. He is the author of three books in the Kogan Page *Books for Teachers* series (on the subjects of the Children Act, truancy, and child protection) and has written numerous articles for newspapers and journals (including *The Guardian, Community Care* and the *Times Educational Supplement*). He has been a regular contributor to components of *The Head's Legal Guide* package and other Croner publications.

He may be available to contribute to local training events, by arrangement with Staffordshire Education Welfare Service. Tel: 01785-278 964.

THE REVIEWER

ANTHONY WOODARD taught for 27 years in maintained secondary schools, becoming Head of a comprehensive secondary school in Surrey. He worked at Croner Publications for several years before finishing his full-time career as Deputy Director of Education for the Archdiocese of Southwark.

He continues as External Editor of Croner's *The Head's Legal Guide* and is secretary to the Education Law Association. He is a governor of a voluntary-aided school in West Sussex.

CONTENTS

NARRATIVE CASE-STUDIES

The Complete Guide to Attendance and Absence

Ben Whitney

Croner Publications Ltd
Croner House
London Road
Kingston upon Thames
Surrey KT2 6SR
Telephone: 0181-547 3333

Published by
Croner Publications Ltd
Croner House
London Road
Kingston upon Thames
Surrey KT2 6SR
Telephone: 0181-547 3333

While every care has been taken
in the writing and editing of this book,
readers should be aware that only Acts of Parliament
and Statutory Instruments have the force of law,
and that only the Court can authoritatively
interpret the law.

British Library Cataloguing-in-Publication Data.
A catalogue record for this book
is available from the British Library.

ISBN 1 85524 472 1

Printed by Creative Print and Design, Wales.

PREFACE

There are few more important tasks for teachers than doing their best to make sure children attend school as much as possible. Promoting regular attendance is part of creating an effective school which is committed to raising the levels of achievement of all its pupils. Children cannot learn if they are absent. Those who have time away from school which could have been avoided put their future prospects at risk and are likely to become increasingly disaffected and alienated both from their peers and the world of work. The longer-term implications of underachievement through absence are incalculable, especially in relation to unemployment and youth justice issues. It is also likely that these young people may in turn prove to be parents with an ambivalent attitude towards their own children's future education.

All school staff, across all key stages, are important in these responsibilities, not least because the majority of teachers are responsible for the day-to-day administration of registration and the following up of absences. Poor procedures at this stage will make an effective response less likely. School policies are essential in establishing good practice among staff, children and parents in order to promote as high a level of attendance as possible. Addressing the issues in a proactive way is likely to prevent greater problems occurring later in the child's educational career. Even if this does not benefit your own school, at least it will help colleagues later. The earlier the intervention, the better for everyone.

As well as the need to deal appropriately with individual cases, the Government has placed extensive legal obligations on schools for recording, reporting and publishing data about absence and attendance — from the legal duty to keep attendance registers through to the data which must be included in the annual report and assisting in legal action taken by the LEA. All teachers need information and awareness if these tasks are to be adequately fulfilled in practice.

Many teaching staff are relatively unprepared for these responsibilities. Despite the centrality of this more pastoral role alongside their formal teaching commitments, many receive little formal training in these duties. Teachers depend almost entirely on the extent to which the schools in which they work prepare them. Some will, as a result, learn bad habits alongside good ones! This book aims to provide a comprehensive resource to promote good practice, which will enable any teacher to have the most up-to-date information available to assist them in these key tasks.

Although the material in this book mainly refers to schools maintained by local authorities, I believe that the good practice outlined in it will be of relevance to all schools. This book takes full account of the key resource from the Department for Education and Employment (DfEE) *School attendance and the role of the Education Welfare Service* and the report from the Social Exclusion Unit on truancy and exclusions, both published in 1998. I have been able to develop the issues much further and try to refer to all the necessary documents and regulations at the appropriate place without inundating the text with references.

At various intervals in the text, key points are summarised. There are also three *Question and Answer* sections dealing with specific points of practice.

There are a few places in which, in all humility, I may differ from the official DfEE line and suggest that their own documents do not necessarily interpret the legal requirements correctly. Where these issues are a matter for honest debate, I try to say so but, in general, I hope my more thorough explanation will help to clarify what is sometimes a confusing uncertainty when rules and regulations have to be applied to the "real world".

Ben Whitney
November 1998

CHAPTER 1

THE LEGAL FRAMEWORK

GENERAL

Since at least the **Education Act 1870**, there has been an assumed sense that education in England and Wales is "compulsory". In the early days, this was, of course, a gradual process of prising children away from the other activities which might occupy them as an alternative and holding parents in some way legally accountable for ensuring that their children received at least an elementary level of instruction. Work, especially within the family (such as farming or other home-based occupations), was the most frequent alternative but there were other, even more exploitative activities, many of which would now be seen as child abuse. Some of these, including prostitution and early motherhood, have seen something of a resurgence in recent years, alongside a continuing, if largely hidden, juvenile workforce which undoubtedly still exists.

It is an open question whether there has ever been a *total* acceptance that education should come first in the lives of all children. It is only a generation since large numbers of children in certain communities went through the system and straight into unskilled (if generally available) work with little or no formal qualification to show for their years in school. Many must have been simply going through the motions. The

1

importance to every child's future prospects of what you do at school is a relatively recent idea. Despite all the current concerns about truancy, levels of attendance were probably no higher 30 years ago than they are today — although it seems to matter more now. Even if a commitment to regular attendance cannot be assumed, it has certainly become the majority view, with an ever-increasing period of time in which the child is required to participate (now up to almost the 17th birthday for many). There has never been greater interest in the issue by Government than at present.

Critics might suggest that if our education system were good enough, then children would want to attend. However, some element of legal encouragement has always been retained and, along with it, the existence of the "School Board Man" (*sic*) and the contemporary LEA equivalent in the Education Welfare/Education Social Work Service, in order to encourage the reluctant. There are, perhaps, more opportunities and even positive incentives not to attend school nowadays than ever before, with the advent of home computers, theme parks, extended holidays, cheap foreign travel and homes where adults are out during the day. An element of inevitable teenage rebellion makes even the most ordered and functional family vulnerable, and even the most stimulating and well-organised school needs to be aware of what may need to be done.

Of course, we all know that there is a sense in which it is entirely "normal" for young people to seek to test the boundaries and to discover what actually happens if they do not fall in with what is expected of them. Much use of attendance and absence procedures is not so big a deal and many situations are capable of relatively easy resolution by prompt action. However, some cases of non-attendance, perhaps an increasing number, are but the tip of an iceberg in which not being at school is the presenting problem which betrays something much greater underneath. There are many vulnerable groups of children who cannot be expected to attend school while all else seems to be in chaos around them. These include those whose families are in crisis, those experimenting with drugs, alcohol or other substances, those with major mental health needs, many children in the public care system, the victims of abuse and of discrimination and those grappling with the implications of homelessness, acute poverty, domestic violence and bullying.

The law seeks to be realistic in recognising that 100% attendance is not necessarily required, allowing for "sickness and other unavoidable cause". Some situations, such as children living in families where the nature of the parents' business requires them to travel from place to place, are given special dispensation. There is considerable discretion, given primarily to Heads but also (to a limited extent) to parents, which enables situations which are less than perfect to be regarded as "satisfactory". Effective management of attendance and absence is not solely about the cold enforcement of regulations but simple justice suggests that there should be some consistency to avoid any suggestion that certain children and families have been subject to sanctions on an arbitrary or prejudicial basis.

There is a further complication in the legal framework in that it has never required that all children must go to school. This is a common misunderstanding and, perhaps, one of our best-kept secrets. Since the beginning of the sense of compulsion, "education" has never been defined solely in terms of "schooling". The requirement to ensure that a child is "properly educated" (see below) allows for the possibility that the education provided may involve neither teacher nor school. Whether or not a child is a "registered pupil" is a *crucial* legal issue, which will be explored in considerable detail below.

This definition is of fundamental importance in knowing what may be reasonably expected of a parent. The principle that they may educate their child "otherwise than at school" is a bedrock of our system. If they do so, they do not have to deliver the national curriculum, nor spend a given number of hours in formal instruction, provided the education is "suitable" to the child's needs. True empowerment of parents may be about exploring alternatives, but, *while they choose that their child be a "registered pupil"*, various obligations apply. Changing this status, whether the initiative is taken by the parent or the school, is of enormous significance.

The focus of this book is, of course, on those who make use of schools but this wider context must always be remembered, especially where any question arises about removing children from the school roll, including permanent exclusion and alternative educational programmes.

LEGAL SOURCES

Summary

Education Act 1996	• Duty on parents
	• Definition of "compulsory school age"
	• School Attendance Order
	• Prosecution of parents.
Children Act 1989	• Education Supervision Order
	• General provisions for the welfare of children.
Education Registration Regulations	• Pupils' Attendance Records Regulations 1991
	• Pupil Registration Regulations 1995
	• Pupil Registration (Amendment) Regulations 1997.

Education Act 1996

Summary

Duty on parents	Parents have a legal duty to ensure that their children of compulsory school age are "properly educated, either at school or otherwise" (s.7).
Definition of "compulsory school age"	Children between the age of five and *the end* of the school year in which they become 16 (the last Friday in June for all pupils) (s.8).
School Attendance Order	An order which requires a parent to register his or her child at a school (s.443).
Prosecution of parents	Where "a registered pupil" fails to attend "regularly" (s.444).

The **Education Act 1996** outlines the basic legal obligations on parents and replaced the relevant sections of the **Education Act 1944** and the **Education Act 1993** with effect from 1 November 1996.

Duty on parents

Section 7 of the Act states that:

the parent of every child of compulsory school age shall cause him to receive efficient full-time education suitable:

(a) to his age, ability and aptitude, and

(b) to any special educational needs he may have, either by regular attendance at school or otherwise.

As noted earlier, this means that children do not have to go to school in order to be properly educated. A number of key words are not defined in more detail — for example, what is required for an education to be "efficient", "full-time" or "suitable"? These terms are open to dispute. It is assumed for legal purposes that any educational programme provided through a school or an LEA, including just a few hours home tuition, will meet these criteria, although some establishments which are not officially "schools" may have to have their programmes approved as education "otherwise", even if they provide a fuller timetable.

If parents take up the "otherwise" option by providing the education themselves (and at their own expense), their provision must be inspected and approved by the LEA. If the LEA is not satisfied and is of the view that the child should be enrolled at a school, a School Attendance Order may be sought (see later in this chapter). There are detailed regulations concerning what a Head must do if parents wish to withdraw their child from a school and educate the child themselves at home (see *Education (Pupil Registration) Regulations 1995* below). Education "otherwise" cannot be a shared arrangement along with education at a school — they are mutually exclusive alternatives (except for specific exceptions where children need to attend special units as part of a school-based programme).

If the parents choose a school, the child must then attend "regularly" but this is also not defined. A child who goes to school only every Monday might be said to be attending "regularly", but the parent is clearly also falling foul of the requirement to ensure the child receives an education "full-time". In effect, this means that any session (half day) on which the child is absent without the defence criteria being met (see below) can be evidence of an offence. The number of offences needed to justify a legal, or even a more pastoral response, is, however, not defined in law.

It is important to note that the legal obligation falls entirely on the parents, not on the child. Children cannot be prosecuted for not going to school — truancy is not an offence. It is absence condoned by parents, or, indeed, about which they are powerless but for which they still have to be held legally responsible, which is the focus of enforcement. This is often overlooked or a phrase such as "taking the child to court" may be used. This is inaccurate and potentially counter-productive. Whatever punitive sanctions may be appropriate in response to a child's poor attendance at school, the law allows no action to be taken against the child in the courts, only against the parents. It has often been suggested that truancy might be made an offence by the child, like shoplifting, but the rhetoric has always given way once the problems of definition have been encountered. This is not to say that missing school may not be a risk factor in care proceedings or an issue in a youth justice setting, but it is not, in itself, an offence for which a child can be punished through the courts.

Definition of "compulsory school age"

The definition of "compulsory school age" changed from 1998, when a single leaving date for *all* children in the relevant age year was introduced (see *Education (School Leaving Date) Order 1997* and DfEE Circular 11/97 *School leaving date for 16 year olds*). *All* those who are 16 on or after 1 September in Year 11 may leave school on the last Friday of the following June. At the other end of the spectrum, children must be educated from the age of five, although technically, parents cannot be required either to admit the child to a school or educate them otherwise until the beginning of the term after their fifth birthday.

Many parents and employers (let alone the pupils) believe that the obligation to educate ends on the child's 16th birthday. This has never been the case in England and Wales, although the position in Scotland is different. Even when there were Easter and May leavers, the 16th birthday only determined which of these two dates was significant. This rule applies to all children, however they have been educated. The exception no longer exists for children who had not been on a school admission register for at least a year prior to their 16th birthday, ie since before their 15th birthday. This exception used to allow a few children who had been on home tuition, or in some care and youth offender establishments, to "leave school" early but it no longer applies.

DfEE Circular 11/97 gives guidance as to how those who may not be taking GCSEs should still be enabled to receive a full-time educational programme up to the leaving date — they do not necessarily have to be present at school all the time but should not be allowed simply to stay at home on "study leave" when they have nothing for which to study. They cannot begin work or move on to Training Credits before the end of June. There is no reason why parents cannot be prosecuted for failing to ensure their child is educated, even if he or she is already 16, if the child has not yet reached the leaving date. There must obviously be some purpose to such action (rather than simply locking the stable door after the horse has bolted).

School Attendance Orders

School Attendance Orders (SAOs) (ss.437–443 of the 1996 Act) are for use only where children are not registered at a school but the LEA takes the view that they should be. They are more properly described as "school registration orders" and have no relevance in the context of a child who is already a registered pupil but who is not attending. They are a difficult resource for LEAs to use, with a long and complicated procedure for giving parents various options first and a series of formalised letters and notices within defined timescales. They are used primarily where children have not been registered at age five, on secondary transfer or where the home education allegedly provided by parents has been judged inadequate.

Parents must first reply to a letter indicating whether they are educating their child "otherwise" than at school. If they do not enrol their child at this point, if they do not reply, or if the LEA does not accept the parents' decision, the parents must then be written to again. At this point, the LEA explains that it is of the view that their child should be registered at a school. The parents are invited to choose a school (at which a place is available) or the LEA may nominate its choice of school. Most parents who reach this stage register their child at one of the schools in response and the process ends. If they do not do so within 15 days, the LEA may serve the order, naming the required school. If parents still do not act at this point, they are committing an offence. Once served, the order remains in force for any subsequent school unless the LEA discharges it. SAOs are rare but not unknown.

At its worst, this procedure can become very long and drawn out, with much potential for dispute about whether parents have genuinely tried to get the child into a school and potential difficulties about whether a suitable school is available. The difficulty of making parents re-admit their child to a school once he or she is no longer a registered pupil makes it *essential* that pupils are not removed from a school's admission register precipitously. Parents cannot be held accountable for the fact that a child is not attending once he or she is no longer a registered pupil and some of these situations can drag on for years without resolution if schools or parents act without proper regard to the regulations (see below).

Prosecution of parents

Parents commit an offence under s.444 of the Act if a registered pupil does not attend "regularly". "Parents" here includes any adult looking after the child, even if they are not actually related, but not staff from public agencies. Those with "parental responsibility" living apart from the child can lawfully be prosecuted, although this is rare. Technically, unless authorised by the school, any absence is an offence. LEAs, acting through the Education Welfare or Education Social Work Service, with the approval of key elected members, can prosecute on the evidence of *unauthorised* absence provided by the school. Cases are heard in the local

Magistrates' Court for the area where the child lives, not necessarily the same LEA in which they go to school.

The maximum fine is £1000 but most are much less than this. Courts must take some account of the parents' ability to pay, although they can impose the maximum fine if a parent does not attend the proceedings, at least to begin with. It is expected that during 1999–2000, a greater range of penalties will become available to the court as a result of the **Crime and Disorder Act 1998**. This may include the use of a parenting order which will place parents (not the child) under an obligation to work with the LEA or a member of the Youth Offending Team to address the question of school attendance, as a means of reducing the likelihood that the child may go on to commit criminal offences in future. (Truancy is seen as a key risk indicator. There is still no actual offence by the child, even in this provision.) This longer-term intervention may, in time, replace the need for Education Supervision Orders (see below) and may mean a considerable change in working practice for LEAs.

The attendance register provides the primary evidence on which the parent can be convicted. School attendance registers are legal documents, which is why they must be kept strictly in accordance with the regulations. It is an offence for the "proprietor" of the school to fail to keep both admission and attendance registers within the requirements of the regulations (s.434(6) of the Act). Heads or key members of staff may be required to account to the court for any discrepancies or mistakes. Any dispute between parents and the LEA about whether, for example, a given absence should have been authorised, will require the personal evidence of the Head in explaining the criteria used. This is why schools *must* have written and consistently applied attendance policies, which enable parents to know what the rules are and which ensure consistent practice by staff (see also *Chapter 2: Effective Registration* and *Model School Attendance Policy* in Chapter 3).

The Head will be required to provide six copies, each personally signed, of the child's attendance record during the relevant "period of complaint". This cannot be a computer printout — the necessary form will be provided by the LEA officer. The period of complaint can go back *no further* than six months from the date the information is laid before the court — 12–15 weeks is usually sufficient. There is no need for unauthorised absence to continue for six months before prosecution is even considered. The Head (or a key member of staff) may also be asked to provide a written statement of evidence outlining the criteria on which the absences have been left unauthorised and any inappropriate explanations provided by the parents. The offence is not difficult to prove, *provided that the grounds for not authorising the absences are clear.*

There are various statutory defences in s.444 on which parents may rely. However, if they appear to have any merit, it is unlikely that the LEA will proceed. Here too, there are major implications for the school's record-keeping. No offence is committed if the child is absent "with leave", granted by someone at the school authorised to grant it, or if parents can prove that the child was absent due to sickness or some other "unavoidable cause". Failure by the LEA to provide transport where required to do so and certain other statutory defences, such as religious festivals, may also be cited.

If the school has an organised approach to registration and is careful to identify unauthorised absence, it should have no difficulty in providing the necessary evidence in such cases. Authorising absences which everyone believes to be inappropriate renders the LEA powerless. The law requires a school to have the courage of its convictions and to place the possible detrimental effect of unauthorised absence on their "league table" figure, *below* the need to demonstrate an intolerance of unreasonable absence. Placing these objectives the other way round means that, while headline unauthorised absence figures may be improved, the school is effectively colluding with individual parents in breaking the law.

The effectiveness of prosecution has never been the subject of any serious research and national statistics about its use are not available from the DfEE. There is a general sense that "good" LEAs are frequent users of the courts, although some would argue that having to prosecute a parent is a sign of failure which is always best avoided if possible. There is no obvious evidence that schools and LEAs which make most use of prosecution also have the best attendance figures — that would in any case be an unfair measure. Neither are they best evaluated by how high the fines are — some of which will not actually be paid or will be reduced on appeal. Prosecution is time-consuming for the individual LEA officer and the best measure of its effectiveness would be whether *that child*, or perhaps that wider family, shows a subsequent improvement in school attendance and performance.

No research is available which can demonstrate the facts one way or the other but all EWOs and Heads will want to reinforce the right messages. Perhaps surprisingly, courts are not always sympathetic to the LEA's actions and parents have plenty of opportunity to plead mitigation, which may mean the initiative is somewhat counter-productive in practice. Clear decision-making procedures must be in place to ensure that cases suitable for prosecution are appropriately identified and the best possible action taken at the best possible time (see *Chapter 4: Interagency Working*). Decisions are often made too late in a child's school career to have any real impact.

Children Act 1989

Summary

Education Supervision Order	Places a child under the supervision of the LEA, on the grounds that he or she is not being "properly educated". Gives LEA power to issue "directions" to child/parent. The parent commits an offence if the order is not complied with.
General provisions for the welfare of children	Family Proceedings Courts should pay attention to a child's "educational needs" when deciding whether or not the child is suffering "significant harm".

(There may be changes to the use of these powers when the **Crime and Disorder Act 1998** is fully implemented and with the proposed use of parenting orders as effectively an alternative/replacement for ESOs.)

Education Supervision Orders

The **Children Act 1989** is the framework for dealing with children who are experiencing family problems, both "private law" (divorce, etc) and "public law" (care proceedings, child protection, etc). The Act, implemented in October 1991, removed the power of the LEA to apply to have a child taken into local authority care for not attending school. Under previous legislation, certain grounds were listed which proved that the child's needs required the acquisition of parental rights by the local authority — absence from school was specifically included, although many of the children remained at home, even if they were under a care order and the cases were often given low priority.

Although, in practice, these powers were normally used only where there were other contributory risk factors, the new concept of "significant harm" has not generally been seen as justifying intervention by the social services department on school attendance grounds as the primary issue, although there have been a few isolated examples. Older children who are refusing to go to school may well be "beyond parental control" but whether the making of a care order will be better for them than no order at all (a key concept of the Act) is often an open question. There has been a move towards working on a non-statutory basis giving rise to concern that this may leave vulnerable and damaged children free to opt out of education entirely if they refuse to co-operate.

Under s.36, absence from school alone is sufficient grounds for an ESO (the issue of authorised/unauthorised absence is not so important in this context), although there is a requirement to try to resolve problems by voluntary means wherever possible. This tends to mean that ESOs are sought only as a last resort and when there is not much hope left of improvement. They are probably better used earlier, after a reasonable attempt at resolution, and work only in situations where the introduction of some external authority may help parents who are struggling to manage the child's education, including those who have failed to educate them "otherwise" to a satisfactory standard. They cannot be used to force anyone to do anything but the Supervisor must "advise, assist and befriend" the child and can give "directions" to the parents and the child in order to ensure that the child is educated.

The orders are made in the Family Proceedings Court (where issues of care, child protection, residence after divorce, etc are also dealt with) and can be applied for only by LEA officers. Heads are required to provide records of the child's attendance at school and a report outlining his or her educational needs and progress. There must be a realistic expectation that the structure of the order is likely to help the situation to improve, so it is vital that there is a clear sense of what the professionals wish to achieve for the child. There has to be an action plan, to which the full commitment of the school is essential. ESOs are not punitive against parents or children but are based on the best hope of promoting their welfare.

The officers managing the order do not provide the education themselves, so there has to be full consultation with schools both before and after the making of the order to ensure that it has a chance of success. Orders last for one year but may be extended in exceptional circumstances. Many LEAs have largely ignored them, either through a lack of clear policy and resources, or because it is not entirely clear when they are best used or whether they add anything useful to complex problems. Allocating a Supervisor to just one child is a major use of an EWO's time and many will feel that they are better used less intensively with a larger number of children (see also *Chapter 4: Inter-agency Working*).

General provisions for the welfare of children

The wider provisions of the Act are also relevant, where a child is considered at risk of "significant harm" to their "health or development" or in dealing with the consequences of abuse and other family problems. Although absence from school alone is not usually grounds for proceedings, action by the social services department on wider grounds could take into account the failure by parents to ensure their child was educated, alongside other issues. The test of "significant harm" is a considerable one, although it might be relevant where a child has special needs which have not been met or where parents are also neglecting their child in other ways. However, social workers may not always be aware of how important education is to a child's well-being.

School staff may also be asked to provide information about a child's educational career in the context of disputes about, for example, where the child should live following divorce, or a dispute between unmarried parents. This can be a difficult area in which staff will naturally be unwilling to be seen to be taking sides but the court may want to know, for example, any information which the school has about past involvement by the parents and their general attitude to education.

The court is supposed to take education into account in *any* decision which may affect the child's welfare. Teachers should not be left to pick up the pieces of, for example, a move to a new carer, without the educational consequences of the decision being anticipated. This is not always considered, however, and parents always have the power to act unilaterally unless there are court orders which specify the arrangements. Teachers should see themselves as key agents in protecting the educational welfare of children, along with colleagues from the LEA, and should co-operate with any request from the social services or the court for information.

Regulations Governing Registration

Note that the **Education (Pupils' Attendance Records) Regulations 1991** amended the 1956 Regulations which were revoked by the **Education (Pupil Registration) Regulations 1995**. The requirement to report absence figures appears, at present, in the **Education (School Information) (England) Regulations 1996**.

Summary

Education (Pupils' Attendance Records) Regulations 1991	• Created the concept of "authorised" and "unauthorised" absence and require every absence to be classified by the school as one or the other • Allowed schools to use computerised registration systems.
Education (Pupil Registration) Regulations 1995	• Require the keeping of registers • Define the circumstances under which children may be removed from the school roll • Procedures for family holidays and other leaves of absence • Inspection of registers by LEA officers • Preservation of registers, etc.
Education (Pupil Registration)(Amendment) Regulations 1997	• Allowed for afternoon registration to be at any time and introduced a new registration category of "approved educational activity".

Education (Pupils' Attendance Records) Regulations 1991

These regulations amended the **Pupils Registration Regulations 1956** by requiring schools to report each year on their absence figures — intially only unauthorised absence but now both authorised and unauthorised. These show the figures up to the end of May, which is the end of the school year for statistical purposes *only*. The regulations also first introduced the concept of computerised registration. The subject of daily registration is covered in greater detail in *Chapter 2: Effective Registration* but it is important to recognise that these regulations define significant areas of legal action concerning the admission and attendance of pupils of compulsory school age who are not boarders.

Regulation 2(2) (now Regulation 7 of the 1995 Regulations) requires a system within every school for identifying which absences are unauthorised. As outlined previously, this decision determines whether or not the parent is committing an offence and so should obviously be made according to clear criteria. Many schools authorise too generously or may never have established clear policies and procedures which are consistently applied across the school. It should be clear whose responsibility it is to make a decision — the class teacher's, the year head's or the Head's — and what procedures are in place for clarifying any uncertainties or challenging parents' explanations for absence.

Unfortunately, as mentioned earlier, the introduction of these regulations has come to be associated with achieving as low as possible a figure for unauthorised absence, rather than providing a focus for defining clear expectations with parents as was the intention. The data provided for the "league tables" is not as important as ensuring that parents and children receive the right signals. Low unauthorised absence does not necessarily mean high attendance — some schools authorise as many as 14% of sessions as legitimate absence, while others authorise only 4%.

It is clear that very different expectations are being applied and the real levels of inappropriate absence may be masked. This is the problem in using only the unauthorised figure as the measure of the problem. Schools addressing their attendance responsibilities and being stricter with parents may see it rise, at least in the short term, which is hardly an incentive. It would probably be better for everyone if *attendance* rather than only certain kinds of absence were the focus. This would enable much fairer comparisons to be made between schools rather than comparing only those absences which each school considers to be unauthorised, according to whatever criteria they each use.

The keeping of attendance records by computer has proved to be a useful tool for many schools and several different systems are available (see also regulation 16 of the 1995 Regulations below). It is important that the use of technology is not seen, in itself, as a solution to problems of poor attendance. It is the interpretation and use of the data which really matters, even allowing for the helpfulness of being able to do the calculations much more easily and the ease of producing an individual pupil's record. It may be extremely helpful, for example, to make a child's attendance history known to the parents on a regular basis and computer printouts are ideal for this purpose.

The regulations require that a "hard copy" is made of a computerised attendance register on a *monthly* basis. These must then be made into bound volumes for the year and form the permanent record of the child's attendance for legal purposes, which, like manual registers, must be kept for at least three years. These printouts *should not be changed* once they have been made. It raises very serious questions about the legality of the record if, for example, the "copy" of the register produced in a court is not, in fact, the same as the record currently held by the school. Exactly when the monthly printout should be made is not specified but it clearly cannot be at the end of the school year. There must be a cut-off point at which absences from the previous month which have not been satisfactorily explained according to the school's procedures must then be *permanently* recorded as unauthorised.

Education (Pupil Registration) Regulations 1995

Maintaining an admission register/school roll (regulations 5–7 and 14–16)

The admission register / school roll may be kept by means of a computer but an annual printout must be made and kept for at least three years. The admission register must include known information about parents as well as the children (including those with parental responsibility living apart from their child). Data collection systems must be set up in a way which asks the right questions on admission and updates the information annually. This should include the school the child last attended, if any, and the admission date. A child cannot be on the admission register but not on the attendance register and there is no such thing as a "trial" admission in which the child attends but is not marked in the registers for a period of time. Once a child has attended for *one session* (half a day), they must be considered to be a "registered pupil" with all the legal implications of that status. This is essential to avoid children being left between, for example, two schools, neither of which accept that he or she is their pupil.

Holiday leave (regulation 8)

Regulation 8 defines the Head's power to grant leave of absence for holidays during term time. There is no automatic entitlement, only discretion to grant leave up to *10 days* per school year if appropriate. The circumstances must be exceptional for any longer to be allowed and application must be made in advance *by the parent with day-to-day care*. The child must be "going away" but the parent does not necessarily have to be going with them. A father not living with the child, or a grandparent, for example, needs the parent with care to make the application on their behalf (see also *Chapter 2: Effective Registration*).

Deletions from the admission register/school roll (regulation 9)

Schools are not free simply to remove children from registers as they wish. Doing so means they are no longer a "registered pupil". It removes entirely the legal obligation on the parent to ensure they attend and leaves the child in "limbo" unless the action is within the regulations. Children cannot be removed from the attendance register but remain on the "school roll". Even those on long-term home tuition, if they are still "registered pupils" who are included within the school's return on Form 7, must receive a mark for each session (see pages 26 and 27 for recommended codes). All those on the admission register must also be in the attendance register — a child cannot be deleted from the attendance register unless he or she is also deleted from the admission register. The most common situations in which children's names may be deleted are outlined below.

1. When the child "has been registered" at another school. Children should not be removed from the register on a "promise" by parents, only when the school is informed *by another school* that they have actually admitted the child (or after four weeks if they have moved away but no subsequent school has been in contact — see below).

2. When parents have given *written* notification to the school that they are educating the child "otherwise" than at school. The school must then inform the LEA's Monitoring Officer who will advise on exactly when the child's name should be deleted. It should not be done

immediately the letter has been received as there will need to be some procedure for verifying that the parents are serious, not merely trying to avoid their educational responsibilities.

3. When the child has stopped attending and no longer "ordinarily resides" at a place which is a reasonable distance from the current school. This does *not* give the school power to remove the name of a child who has stopped attending but who is still living at the same address. It only covers children who have physically moved their home address. If there is no contact from any other school, the LEA/EWO *must* be informed so that checks can be made about whether the child has been admitted elsewhere.

4. When the child has not returned within 10 more school days after exceptional leave of absence (extra long holiday), except by virtue of illness or other unavoidable cause. These children may reasonably be assumed not to be coming back so that the school does not have to carry the absences. (It may be best to remove children from the roll when they go abroad for extended periods on the grounds that they are now "ordinarily resident" abroad, if the trip is expected to be long or is open-ended. The child could then be re-admitted on returning to the UK.)

5. After four weeks continuous absence *and* "both the proprietor of the school and the local education authority have failed, after reasonable enquiry, to locate the pupil." This is for use *only* where the pupil has disappeared/moved to an unknown address, not for situations where he or she is refusing to attend but still resident in the same place. The school cannot act without consultation with the LEA first to make a joint decision. The 1998 guidance from the DfEE repeats the statement that exclusion is not an appropriate response to absence and simply removing the child from the roll as an alternative is illegal.

6. At the end of the process of any permanent exclusion (ie not until all necessary representations have been made to the governors and, if applicable, to the LEA and the appeal process has been completed, not from the day of the exclusion itself).

Other situations cover where the pupil has died, or is judged permanently medically unfit for school, or where he or she ceases to be of compulsory school age. This does not give the parents power to remove the child immediately he or she becomes 16. Deletions outside these rules usually cause ongoing problems for everyone. All of this is intended to ensure that there are no children whose status is unclear or who are "lost" to the system. This is how children end up not receiving any education for years on end, with all the dire consequences this brings. LEAs need to be able to check on the whereabouts of children who are out of the system. Where children are not in school, it must be clear which are registered pupils but absent and which are supposedly being educated in some other way. There should be no other alternatives.

Dual registration (regulation 10)

Children should not normally be on the registers of two schools at once but there are circumstances (particularly involving special schools, Pupil Referral Units and assessment centres) where dual registration may be needed. The 1997 (Amendment) Regulations also allow for special arrangements for traveller children (see below).

Inspection of registers and making copies (regulations 11 and 12)

Maintained schools must make their registers available for inspection by authorised officers of the LEA. *All* schools must do so for OFSTED and other inspectors. These officers must also be permitted to make copies for courts, etc.

Education (Pupil Registration) (Amendment) Regulations 1997

Traditionally, registers have always had to be marked at the beginning of each half-day session. This is still the requirement for the morning session but, from 1 January 1998, the DfEE decided to give schools flexibility about when they can mark afternoon registers. This raises a number of potential problems.

1. If attendance registers are not marked immediately after lunch, it is impossible for the staff or an EWO to know during the afternoon session whether or not a given child is in school, without having to check individually.

2. It is impossible for a child to be late if the register is not called at the beginning of the session, thus rendering all the rules about lateness irrelevant.

3. A child could go missing for almost six hours and the absence would not be officially noted.

As the DfEE advised at the time, schools choosing later registration arrangements for the afternoon will have to have additional systems, eg for fire purposes and for checking that children have not left at lunchtime. There are also some doubts about whether absence at the end of the session will be proof of an offence if a parent claims that the child was present at school at the beginning of the session. This has yet to be tested in the courts.

All of this may suggest that there is no value in making this change and that it will only cause other difficulties. The same expectations should apply in every school. There is no need for any flexibility about what is a universal duty which should treat every parent and child in the same way.

More importantly, these regulations also introduced a fourth registration category alongside "present", "authorised absent" and "unauthorised absent" (see *Chapter 2: Effective Registration*). Many schools will already have been counting those who are away from the premises for legitimate reasons (such as an educational visit) as "present" for statistical purposes (although the DfEE says that children marked in this way are technically neither present nor absent).

The previous regulations classed all those not on the premises as "authorised absent", even if the child was where he or she was supposed to be. This was plainly unreasonable. The new arrangement introduced the concept of an "approved educational activity". This covers:

- approved work experience for older pupils
- field trips and educational visits
- approved sporting activities
- link courses/FE colleges
- "franchised" pupils receiving part of their education at another school or unit while remaining the responsibility of the school where registered.

This change is *not* intended to cover children who have been placed on home tuition while remaining a registered pupil, such as those with a long-term illness. They still have to be classed as authorised absent as the amount of education they will be receiving is not considered sufficient or under the day-to-day supervision of a teacher. This even applies to children attending hospital schools or receiving tuition in hospital where their status as ill is seen by the DfEE as dominant — they too must still be classed as authorised absent.

Those children who are covered by this arrangement should be shown in the register by a suitable code *without* an "O" in order to distinguish them from authorised absences. They are now officially counted as "present" for the purposes of the annual DfEE returns — computerised systems will need to be adjusted to record the totals appropriately. This system should have been been in place from 1 January 1998 (although the computer software was initially not available). It is essential for schools to have procedures in place which check that the pupil actually attended as required. This coding system cannot be a blanket arrangement to class a pupil as present in sessions in which the pupil did not comply with an agreed arrangement — these would still be *unauthorised* absences.

These regulations also contain clarification of the position regarding traveller children. There is concern about the possibility of losing track of children, some of whom might not be in education elsewhere or, in rare cases, where their welfare might be at risk. The provision for parents whose business requires them to travel with their family is not intended to allow them to educate their children only on a part-time basis. A new authorisation code, "O" with a "T" inserted, is suggested as a way of keeping children on the roll while temporarily away from their usual school base. This would also facilitate better arrangements for distance learning but should not be seen as a long-term alternative to school attendance. These arrangements will be classed as an authorised absence and the children cannot be counted as present.

CONCLUSION

Within the variety of legal sources discussed in this chapter, it is possible to discern certain values which, while not always entirely consistent with one another, need to be held alongside each other in ensuring good practice in dealing with attendance and absence issues.

Valuing Education

The Government believes that all children should have the opportunity to benefit from their education. Ensuring school attendance is not optional for parents once their children become registered pupils — it is a key part of their parental duty.

Education makes an important contribution to reducing "social exclusion" and teenage delinquency. Schools are accountable for the levels of attendance of their pupils in order to ensure that children's right to education is not overlooked.

Sharing in Partnership

While the LEA has the final responsibility for ensuring that the legal duty on parents is carried out, these joint responsibilities are best approached in partnership with all those involved. This includes the school, the parents, the child, the LEA and any other relevant agencies with an interest in the welfare of children.

Working by Agreement

When problems arise, an approach based on securing the co-operation of parents through negotiated agreements should be attempted wherever possible. The use of courts is restricted to situations where the welfare of the child is at risk or where parents have persistently failed to act responsibly.

CHAPTER 2

EFFECTIVE REGISTRATION

GENERAL

The information in this chapter should be considered in conjuction with the various regulations (see *Chapter 1: The Legal Framework*) and the guidance issued by the DfEE in 1998 *School attendance and the role of the Education Welfare Service*.

Marking registers properly is fundamental to a whole-school approach to promoting attendance but many schools have not formulated clear procedures for staff or made them known to parents. Registration practice should be a key part of a school's written attendance policy, alongside strategies for rewarding attendance, appropriate responses to unauthorised absence and effective working relationships with parents and other professionals.

A key to good practice is to set aside a clear time for registration. This is an important part of the school day, not merely an administrative routine. Registration is required by law at the *beginning* of each morning session and at some point during the afternoon session (in practice, this is normally the beginning).

Registration should be a significant expression of the school's care for the pupils and is a useful time for the sharing of information and the reinforcement of the need for parental notes after an absence. The marking of registers should never be delegated to a pupil. Registers are an essential legal document, whether kept manually or by computer and the quality of registration is often an indicator of a school's awareness of wider attendance issues.

It is essential to be consistent in the definitions used of authorised and unauthorised absence. Parents and children should not be faced with differing expectations according to who is marking the register. In particular, there must be a *standard system* for recording absences, especially the codes entered in the registers to indicate on what grounds absences have been authorised by the school (unauthorised absences, except lateness after registration, contain no code). A provisional mark can be entered, to be clarified later in the light of further information, although this should *not* result in the wholesale authorisation of previously blank noughts many months later, simply on the parent's signature.

RECOMMENDED ATTENDANCE REGISTER SYMBOLS

The codes below are those recommended for use from January 1998.

Manual Registers

It is important to note that computerised registers must be set up to show the same information, although they might not use the same symbols and codes.

There are now *four* registration categories.

1. *Present.* Denoted by a forward or reverse oblique (/ or \).
2. *Approved educational activity.* Denoted by a letter with no "O" (see table below).
3. *Authorised absent.* Denoted by "O" with the appropriate letter inserted (see table below).

4. *Unauthorised absent*. Denoted by "O" with no letter inserted (except for lateness after registration).

Approved educational activity (no "O")	
Approved sporting activity	P
School visits and field trips	V
Work experience	W
Link courses at FE colleges and children receiving part of their education "off site"	Z
Authorised absence ("O" with the appropriate letter inserted)	
Absent for "performance" licensed by LEA	A
Pupil attending another school/unit and being marked there	B
Special circumstances not covered elsewhere	C
Exclusion — fixed term and permanent awaiting confirmation	E
Family holiday in term time (10 days maximum)	H
Attending interview	I
Illness/medical (absent for whole session)	M
Day of religious observance	R
Study leave (Year 11 pupils only)	S
Traveller absence (children expected to return to school)	T
Unauthorised absence	
No satisfactory explanation received	"O" with *no* code
Lateness	
Late *within* the registration period or for an acceptable reason (present)	"O" overmarked with a / or \
Late *after* the registration period or without acceptable reason (unauthorised absent)	"O" with L inserted

Monitoring attendance is not only about putting the appropriate mark in the register. DfEE returns should be completed accurately and on time; problems should be identified at the earliest possible stage. Schools must be vigilant in detecting truancy after registration and individual children may require additional monitoring on a lesson-by-lesson basis. It is important that records are totalled accurately and that appropriate entries are made in the registers, if kept manually.

AUTHORISING ABSENCE

Deciding whether the absence is authorised is the school's responsibility, not the parents'. The attendance policy should make this absolutely clear. Each authorised absence must contain the relevant code for that half-day session. The majority of authorised absences will be for sickness but the Head and governors should ensure that clear guidance is given to staff and that agreed procedures are actually followed. Senior staff should regularly monitor the practice of those with day-to-day responsibility and ensure that any uncertainties are dealt with properly (see the *Checklist* at the end of this chapter).

Care should be taken in the school's use of this discretion to authorise absence. At its worst, this power can lead to a school effectively colluding with parents in allowing children to be absent when they should have attended.

Normally, only *unavoidable* absences should be authorised. This does not mean that any explanation, however inappropriate, which is offered by a parent must be accepted as grounds for authorisation. A note, in itself, is not sufficient — it depends on what the note says. If authorisation is used over-generously, this may send a signal to parents and children that attendance is not important and that obtaining authorisation is easy.

Clear procedures should be in place, especially where staff feel that too many absences are being accounted for by parental notes. It is quite acceptable (indeed it is good practice) to indicate to the parents that absences will not be authorised in future without some additional assurance that the absences were unavoidable. There is no obligation to authorise on request. This may lead to an increase in unauthorised absence — it will almost certainly also lead to an increase in attendance, (the primary objective) as parents and pupils come to see that the school will not simply grant permission without question.

Defining "unavoidable" Absence From School

In 1997, Lincolnshire LEA prosecuted a parent for failing to ensure that her daughter attended school. The defence argued that the cause of the pupil's absence was "unavoidable" because she had a child of her own to look after. The parent's argument was accepted and the case was dismissed.

Aside from the question of whether it is reasonable to expect children of compulsory school age who become mothers also to attend school (and there are usually alternatives which can adequately satisfy legal requirements), the case raises the importance of the fact that absence due to an "unavoidable cause" is not an offence (**Education Act 1996** s.444(3)(b)). Parents do not commit an offence simply because the pupil is absent and the question of definition will often determine whether or not an LEA has any power to take proceedings against them.

Consider, for example, the persistent "truant", ie the child who chooses either to be absent from school on a regular basis or who fails to stay at school for the whole day. Such an absence may be avoidable in the sense that the child could have chosen otherwise but parents (who are the only ones who can commit the offence, not the pupil) might successfully argue, especially in relation to an older child, that they had done everything reasonable to avoid the situation.

Reasonable steps would include waking the child in time to go to school, providing the uniform and dinner money, telephoning the school to check the child had arrived, even taking the child to school or responding immediately every time the school alerted them to the child going missing. All such strategies might fail and the child refuse to co-operate. If, despite the parents' best efforts, the child still fails to attend, such absence might meet the test of "unavoidable" absence as far as the parents are concerned. Courts, however, do not usually accept such an argument — parents have to carry the can even if they feel powerless. It is the school rather than the parent which normally determines which absences are acceptable and which are not but such judgments must be open to scrutiny as fair in all the circumstances.

The case outlined above should cause school staff to reflect on the way in which they authorise pupils to be absent. In doing so, they are recognising that the "unavoidable" criteria apply and that no offence occurs. There are basically only two grounds for authorising an absence; the regulations distinguish between "leave" and being "unable to attend".

1. "Leave" granted *by the school*, ie situations where the child is not required to attend, such as exclusions, study leave, family holidays, children licensed by the LEA to appear in an entertainment, school closures, etc. These are largely defined by regulations where the school is required to grant leave if the appropriate criteria apply (although some, eg family holidays, contain an element of discretion).

2. Explanations for absence provided *by the parents* which are accepted by the school as "unavoidable", such as illness, emergencies, bad weather and some lateness, etc. These are much more a matter of the parents taking the initiative in keeping the child off school and the school having to decide whether or not to accept their explanation.

Deciding What is Acceptable

Both of the above categories require each school to have a clear sense of what is acceptable and to make this very clear to parents. In the case of the young mother, for example, many schools might have authorised the absences on the grounds that she could not reasonably be expected to attend. They may have sent work home, or agreed with the LEA that home tuition be provided, at least at first. There could then have been no prosecution as there would have been no evidence.

Only absences which *the school* judges to be unavoidable are relevant to whether an offence is being committed by the parents. The LEA may advise but it is not its decision. The evidence produced is an exact copy of the school register, marked in accordance with the school's attendance policy and for which the Head is accountable in the event of any dispute.

It is vital that schools do not describe absences as "unavoidable", and therefore authorise them, too readily. It is not the note provided by the parent which gives grounds for this decision, it is the explanation the note gives. Even with quite significant health problems, a child might still be reasonably expected to attend. Children with temporary injuries or with minor fractures can often still be accommodated at school. The intention of the legislation is that there must be no reasonable way in which the child could have managed to come to school before the absence should be authorised.

This means that a whole range of possible reasons for absence should not be accepted automatically — it depends on the circumstances. Staying at home to look after younger siblings would not normally qualify as unavoidable but it might be if the child is also a carer for a parent with a disability or in an emergency. Shopping rarely has to be done during school time and day trips might reasonably wait for weekends and holidays, although there might be extenuating circumstances when, perhaps, relatives are visiting from abroad or the child has won a prize. Some absences are reasonable, especially if the child is normally a good attender, even if they are not strictly "unavoidable".

However, the published absence figures still suggest that many schools are authorising absences too generously. It is difficult to see how absence from an average of 10% or more sessions across a whole school can be "unavoidable", even allowing for 'flu epidemics and other local circumstances, though some high figures might result from the reluctant acceptance of unresolvable situations.

Clarifying School Attendance Policies

Written school attendance policies should make it clear that the school will not accept just *any* explanation as grounds for authorisation, only those where the absence could not reasonably have been avoided. Any dispute about this in court will have to be referred to the Head, who would have to appear in person to explain the basis of the decision. A parent may always query the decision of the school not to authorise absence if they maintain that the absence was unavoidable, so the grounds for decision-making must be clear.

It is advisable to operate according to very clear criteria, which are applied equally and consistently and with as few people as possible exercising a measure of judgment where there is any uncertainty. Experience suggests that such a "strict" approach to authorising only unavoidable absence leads to parents who are less likely to offer inadequate explanations and to increased rates of actual attendance once the school's expectations are clear.

Special Circumstances

There are other circumstances where the school may wish to exercise some discretion to allow a child to be absent. Bereavement of a family member or close friend is often grounds for authorising absence, although staff should guard against children being away for more than a day or two unless the circumstances are exceptional.

Some children are juggling school with responsibilities as carers, or suffering from persistent periods of difficulty with their physical or mental health. These will normally be reasonable grounds. Schools will, however, need to be wary of parents requesting time away from school for their children to take part in entertainments, modelling, film and television work. This can be highly lucrative and can benefit the child in many ways but leave should not be allowed unless the LEA has issued the necessary licence. Circumstances covered by authorisation code "C" are intended to be out of the ordinary, such as a wedding or other special occasion, not just because it is the child's birthday, for example. There may need to be a procedure for making these decisions so that different form teachers do not apply very different standards.

There will always be exceptions to every rule but schools should be careful not to give the impression that authorisation is ever simply a matter of routine.

PUNCTUALITY AND LATENESS

Section 7 of the **Education Act 1996** requires parents to ensure that their child receives "efficient, *full-time* education, either at school or otherwise". This raises key questions about the definition of "full-time" and the way in which schools record the data relating to children whose punctuality is poor.

The case of *Hinchley v Rankin* [1961] established that late arrival could still be seen as absence but many schools have yet to develop a coherent policy on this issue and many operate inconsistent or unclear procedures. Since this case, further complications have been added by the creation of authorised and unauthorised absences under the **Education (Pupils' Attendance Records) Regulations 1991** (SI 1991/1582) and the **Education (Pupil Registration) Regulations 1995** which revoked them. Some kinds of lateness will be acceptable, such as those due to an early morning medical appointment, adverse weather conditions or the failure of school transport. Schools need to make a clear distinction between those late arrivals which are legitimate and those which are not and to show that distinction in the register by the appropriate use of different codes.

It must be the school, not the parents or the pupil, which defines the attendance times that will be considered appropriate. Clearly there is room for some discretion to take account of individual circumstances but unacceptable lateness *must* be classified as "unauthorised absence" if LEAs are to use such failure as evidence for prosecution. Late arrival which the school has accepted as reasonable cannot then be used against the parent. It is vital that appropriate symbols are used to distinguish between the two and that totals are reckoned accordingly.

What Constitutes Lateness?

It is the responsibility of each educational establishment catering for children of compulsory school age to define in its attendance policy what the expectations of the governing body are. Such expectations should also be widely published and reinforced, to staff, parents and pupils. There must be consistency across the school or there is little chance of developing a whole-school identity on the issue. Differing expectations will confuse parents and make legal action unnecessarily arbitrary.

In deciding whether lateness is reasonable, a key issue concerns whether or not the child arrives during or after the period of time at the beginning of the session which is set aside for registration. (If afternoon registration is not at the beginning of the session, a child cannot be late — he or she must be counted as present if they are there when the register is called no matter when they arrived.)

Schools are free to decide how long the registration period lasts, depending on their circumstances but it cannot be an open-ended period which lasts for the whole time the school is open.

For example, a primary school serving a local area where every child lives within walking distance might hold that an arrival time of no longer than 10 or 15 minutes is reasonable. A school where children travel from a wide area and where the vagaries of traffic and public transport might reasonably come into play could allow longer. The DfEE, in the key booklet on these and other registration issues *School attendance and the role of the Education Welfare Service* (1998) indicated that 30 minutes could be seen as a reasonable maximum. Afternoon times could be considerably shorter. Once the period of registration is defined, unacceptable arrival outside these times would constitute "absence" and could therefore be used as evidence, provided such lateness is classified by the school as unauthorised.

Procedures

Registration procedures need to make it clear in the register for each given case which kind of lateness it is. For example, pupil A is not present when his name is called, so an "O" is entered in the register. He arrives, however, before the end of the time set aside for registration, so the "O" is overmarked with an oblique (/) and the child can be credited with an attendance and counted as present.

This is not to say that no effort should be made to encourage the child to attend a little earlier but the parents cannot be said to have failed in their legal duty in this situation. The longer the school allows for legitimate registration of this kind, the greater the freedom being accorded to parents.

Child B, however, also absent when the register was called, arrives mid-morning without reasonable excuse, well after the registration period has ended. It is important to show that this child is now on the premises after some signing-in procedure (for fire safety purposes, etc) but this late arrival cannot be counted as a legal attendance. The "O" in the register should have the letter L added and this session be counted as unauthorised absence.

Anything other than an occasional example should be the subject of information to the parents, making it clear that such late arrival is no different from no attendance at all and that legal action could be taken against them on this basis. Similar distinctions are required where registration is done by means of a computer.

This does raise some difficulties for schools. In the short term, these procedures might increase the number of unauthorised absences and might be seen as reflecting badly on the school. They are likely to lead to greater conflict with parents if standards have previously been unclear. But it is impossible to see the lateness as a problem one minute but count it as a legitimate attendance the next. Parents would rightly ask why they are being pestered if the child's attendance record still shows the lateness as acceptable. It is to be hoped that, in the longer term, a stricter line on punctuality will lead to improved levels of full-time attendance.

These requirements may also lead some parents and pupils to suggest that there is no point in coming in at all if half a session is not to be credited as an attendance. However, it might equally be said that there is no point in arriving on time if coming in at any time is still counted as present. This is most unfair on all those pupils and parents who do ensure that they are there when the register is marked.

The most important point is that policy and practice within the school must be clear and consistent. If schools have never indicated in writing to parents and pupils what the expectations are, they cannot be expected to conform to them. If rules are inconsistently applied, an unclear signal will be sent. If schools wish their pupils to attend on time and if parents who fail to make sure they do so without reasonable excuse are to be identified and challenged, there must first be attention to these issues before action by the LEA can be considered as a possibility.

FAMILY HOLIDAYS IN TERM TIME

The amount of time off which children have for holidays in term time is a matter of considerable concern. In many schools it amounts in total to as many authorised absences as are accounted for by illness. There is a general assumption amongst many school staff and parents that such requests must be allowed automatically. However, this is not the case. It should be common practice in every school to spell out exactly on what grounds authorisation will be given or refused. All leave for holidays in term time is discretionary, not an automatic entitlement.

Legislation

The basic framework is regulations 8(3) and 8(4) of the **Education (Pupil Registration) Regulations 1995** (SI 1995/2089), which state the following.

3. Subject to paragraph (4), on application made by a parent with whom the pupil normally resides, a pupil may be granted leave of absence from school to enable him to go away on holiday.

4. Save in exceptional circumstances, a pupil shall not in pursuance of paragraph (3) be granted more than 10 school days leave of absence in any school year.

This Regulation is supplemented by a booklet of guidance from the DfEE *School attendance and the role of the Education Welfare Service* (1998). These provide sufficient information for any school to formulate an appropriate policy. Schools *may* grant holiday leave but they are not required to do so.

Any request to the school for leave should be made in advance. Holidays cannot be authorised retrospectively unless there is a particular reason. It is also the intention of the regulation that this discretion on the part of the school to grant leave, relates to "going away" on holiday. It is not intended to cover authorising children to take day trips or to take a holiday at home. This may cause some difficulty where parents cannot afford to go away but leave might reasonably be refused outside these parameters. It may cause other problems if children who have been given leave by the school to be on "holiday" are actually still in the vicinity or having days out while their neighbours and friends are still expected to attend school.

Requests by Parents

The request should be made by the parent "with whom the pupil normally resides" although the regulation does not specify that the child must be going on holiday with that person. This is intended to cover the situation of children whose parents are separated or divorced or who are going on holiday with someone else or in organised groups. This is very important. The parents may be in dispute about the child and whether the holiday is appropriate. It could cause considerable difficulty if a school grants a request from another person without the knowledge and consent of the parent with day-to-day responsibility for getting the child to school.

The parent with care must make the request on behalf of their estranged partner if they consent to the holiday, even if they are not going on it themselves (eg a holiday with grandparents). It is not appropriate to grant each parent a separate holiday if, in so doing, the total amounts to more than 10 days in the school year, unless the circumstances are exceptional.

Granting Requests

Whether or not to grant the request is a decision for the school. Any absence which is authorised by the school cannot then be used by the LEA as grounds for any offence by the parent. The school's attendance policy should spell out the normal circumstances under which leave will, or will not, be granted.

Guidance from the DfEE says that in the case of family holidays, each case should be considered on its merits — there should not be a "blanket" system of automatic approval. However, schools may wish to make general rules, such as no leave in years 10 and 11, during examinations or in SATs weeks. It may be agreed that a maximum of one week is sufficient under normal circumstances. If such rules are agreed as the school's policy, all absences taken without prior approval or which do not fit the criteria must then be marked as unauthorised absence.

It is especially important not to grant holiday leave where children already have a poor record of attendance. This tends to undermine the efforts of those trying to help the family to see that the child should be in school more regularly. If a child has missed a lot of time, it sends a very ambiguous signal if requests for leave are authorised without question. There is no requirement to authorise just because a request has been made. While this may lead to a short-term increase in the numbers of unauthorised absences, it should also lead to an improved level of attendance, where holidays were previously taken without scrutiny. Many parents take what they see as their entitlement for granted but they may respond positively to stricter expectations, especially if they are applied consistently and fairly.

Some schools have seen a dramatic reduction in the number of requests once it was pointed out that authorisation would not be given automatically. Many parents only ask for leave because they assume it is routinely available. Those children attended when they would otherwise have been absent, potentially making a significant impact on the school's overall rate of attendance.

Requests Totalling more than 10 Days

Requests totalling more than 10 days per school year should be subject to individual approval by the Head. Schools may wish to offer parents the opportunity to make representations to justify their request or involve the governing body in the decision. Some trips are a once in a lifetime chance which may bring considerable educational benefit to the child, such as an extended visit to relatives abroad. Consideration should be given to how the trip may be used as part of an educational programme, perhaps by setting work to be done while away or asking for a project to be submitted on return.

Children leaving the country to visit family, where there is any uncertainty about the date of their return, may be better dealt with outside these regulations. Unless there is any doubt about a place being available later, it is probably more appropriate to remove the child from the roll immediately on departure and to re-enrol them on their return, thus avoiding potentially large numbers of authorised absences.

Requests for other Purposes

Staff need to be especially wary about requests for holidays which are actually for other purposes, such as working in the family business, going fruit-picking, avoiding some part of the school's programme such as a field trip, because of family problems, etc.

Other categories of "leave" should be used if the request is reasonable. No leave should be given to enable the child to work in school time or if the grounds are spurious. Of course, parents may lie and staff are not detectives but experience has shown that reasonable vigilance and clear expectations can have a significant effect in both creating an appropriate climate and in actually improving attendance. No school wants to be seen as a "soft touch" and clear, written procedures are in everyone's interests.

MARKING REGISTERS — QUESTIONS AND ANSWERS

Q. **Must there be an entry in the register for every session?**

A. Yes, for all pupils of compulsory school age. If it has been agreed that the pupil is only required to attend school part-time, there must be an authorised absent mark (or one denoting an alternative educational activity) for all the other sessions.

Q. **Can the same class register be marked by different teachers?**

A. Yes, provided they all use the same system!

Q. **Can the mark in a register be altered?**

A. Yes, provided that the original mark can still be seen. Entries must not be made in pencil, however and correction fluid must *never* be used. Computerised registers record all changes and when they were made.

Q. **Who decides whether an absence is authorised?**

A. This is decided by the school, according to its internal procedures and policy. Advice may be sought from the LEA, information requested from parents, doctors and others but only the school *decides* whether or not to accept the explanation. This is essentially the Head's responsibility (acting in accordance with policy laid down by the governors on the advice of the LEA/DfEE) but it may be delegated to other staff.

Q. **What is the procedure if there is doubt about the parent's explanation for an absence?**

A. Do not authorise the absence without seeking further information first. Of course, it is possible for parents and pupils to mislead deliberately but if there is any doubt, leave the absence unauthorised, at least in the short term. This is especially important if the parents have frequently provided trivial explanations for regular absences or if the grounds given do not seem to merit the length of time away from school. Parents can be asked to provide independent verification of sickness, for example, but doctors may charge for this. Some parents and doctors are willing to make agreements that schools or EWOs can check whether a child has been seen at the surgery, within the limits of confidentiality about the exact reasons. Some doctors will be willing to give an opinion on whether the child is fit for school or how long the child should be absent, without actually breaking confidentiality about the cause.

Q. **Does the school have to accept the parent's note?**

A. No. The information provided by parents is to help the school decide. It can be ignored if the note does not provide a reasonable explanation. The school should keep all notes if there is any likelihood of prosecution. They can be produced in evidence if they provide trivial explanations (or they could be requested by the defence if the parent claims that the child was absent for a legitimate reason which should have been authorised).

Q. **Do explanations from parents have to be in writing?**

A. No. However, telephone explanations are more open to misunderstanding. If notes are not provided, this could cause problems in the event of a dispute. Best practice is for the parent to contact the school by telephone on the first day of absence and then to send a note on the child's return. This also guards against the possibility that the child may be truanting without the parent's knowledge. The note must be from the parent/carer for the child unless the circumstances are exceptional (eg a parent who cannot write).

Q.   **What about trips to the dentist or doctor?**

A.   These are not absences at all unless the child misses the *whole* session. A pupil who goes to the doctor and then comes into school later in the morning can be credited with an attendance for the whole session provided they have attended at the first possible opportunity — this is "acceptable lateness". The situation is similar if a child leaves school after registration for a good reason, such as illness or to attend a hospital appointment. Neither authorised nor unauthorised marks should be used in these circumstances, provided the parents provide a reasonable explanation. Whole sessions missed should be marked as "O" with a letter M inserted as authorised absence, in the same way as for any other sickness absence — the rest count as present.

Q.   **What about absences for minding the house or looking after brothers and sisters?**

A.   These would not normally be grounds for authorising absence, although in an emergency, such as the parent's illness or where the child has ongoing caring responsibilities due to parental disability, special arrangements would be needed. The aim should always be to have the child in school as much as possible. If extended absences are needed, work should always be sent home for the child to do or tuition be offered at the child's home.

Q.   **Is shopping a valid reason for absence?**

A.   Hardly ever!

Q.   **What about day trips?**

A.   Day trips during school time should not normally be authorised as holiday leave and, in general, the DfEE is against them. It might be reasonable to allow the odd day to be authorised for the child who has otherwise attended satisfactorily, though some schools do not grant leave at all for these purposes. While such occasional days should then be marked as unauthorised absences and may spoil the child's otherwise excellent record, there is really nothing that can be done about them if they are only an isolated event, so there is probably little point in making a fuss if the child is usually a good attender.

Q. **Can children have time off for modelling, show rehearsals and performances?**

A. Such requests are becoming more common, along with chances to be in a television programme or times when children are needed for filming, advertisements, etc. This area is regulated by the LEA under the **Children (Performances) Regulations 1968** and school staff should *always* check whether the LEA's permission is required. Absence for amateur productions and one-off television programmes is at the Head's discretion. Professional work must be licensed by the LEA and only the LEA can give permission for the child to be away from school. Most operate on a maximum number of days absence allowed in a six-month period and may have different limits according to the age of the child. These are authorised absences ("O" with an A inserted) if permission is given.

Q. **What about jobs and work experience during school time?**

A. Absence should never be authorised for a child to work and any information known to the school should be reported to the LEA for further investigation. Employers must have a licence to employ even their own children and they cannot work in school hours under any circumstances. Children on work experience placements must be in their final two years of compulsory education and the placement must be approved and supervised by the school under whatever arrangements apply locally. There is no defined limit to how much work experience a child may have. Two weeks is usual but longer arrangements or a regular day each week is legal. Work experience is now an "approved educational activity" and not an authorised absence. (This category is also used for sporting events, field trips and school visits, etc.)

Q. **Must a child be given a day off for a religious festival?**

A. Yes. In these circumstances, schools must grant leave on request. This is one of the specific exemptions in the **Education Act 1996** and it applies to all religious festivals, not only Christian ones. However, requesting a day off each Friday for example, is not reasonable.

Q. **What about a traveller child who only attends school very infrequently?**

A. If the child is currently resident locally, he or she should attend school like any other child, (unless education "otherwise" procedures have been agreed). However, the law allows a child to be absent if his or her parent's business requires them to move from place to place, provided the child attends at least 200 sessions in 12 months (about half time). This should not be used to allow a traveller child to have time off automatically. Such a child may be registered at more than one school — this means he or she will have to be marked authorised absent from school A when travelling legitimately or attending school B. Close liaison should take place with the relevant Traveller Support Service for your LEA area.

Q. **When should a permanently excluded pupil be taken off the register?**

A. Only at the *end* of the exclusion process, including any appeal, not on the actual day of the exclusion. During all this time, as with short-term exclusions, the register should be marked "O" with the letter E inserted and counted as authorised absent.

Q. **Can all Year 11 pupils be given study leave after Easter?**

A. Provided they have exams for which to study, this is authorised absence. The DfEE is less comfortable with pupils being given leave to study when they are not entered for any examinations and such students should be expected to undertake an alternative programme, some of which could be classed as an approved educational activity and which need not necessarily be on the school premises. All Year 11 pupils should receive a mark for each session up to and including the last Friday in June — no-one can "leave school" before this date.

Q.   **What do I put in the register if it snows and half the children do not come in?**

A.   If the school is closed to all pupils, no marks need be entered in the register at all other than "school closed". The special circumstances code ("O" with a C inserted) could be used if it is accepted that attendance was impossible for some individuals even though some children came in. It is important to make it clear to parents whether or not the school is open in the event of bad weather or some other disaster such as frozen pipes or a flood.

Q.   **What about pre-school children and sixth formers?**

A.   The authorised / unauthorised system only applies to children of compulsory school age. For other age groups, registration simply records when the child / young person is on the premises.

Register Inspection Checklist

Admission Register:

- Are all children in both the admission and attendance registers?
- Is all the data complete?
  - name of child, sex, date of birth, date of admission, previous school?
  - parental details (including those with parental responsibility who live elsewhere)
  - emergency contacts
- Any inappropriate deletions? Is LEA informed of deletions? (grounds defined in Education (Pupil Registration) Regulations 1995)

Attendance Register (manual):

- Is the data entered at front (copy of classlist with addresses etc or written in)? (not legally required but considered good practice)
- Are the weekly columns dated etc?
- Is there a mark for each pupil for every session?
- Do absences show a clear distinction between authorised and unauthorised?
- Are the grounds for authorisation clear?
  - coding system used appropriately
  - consistency between registers (school policy / guidance?)
  - criteria for holidays, leave etc (used appropriately?)
  - procedure on lateness — distinguishing before and after registration?
- Are entries in ink and kept neatly?
- Are corrections distinguishable from the original?
- Is the data counted correctly?
- Are children with attendance problems being properly identified and appropriate responses made — school-based and referral to LEA?
- Are the registers kept for at least three years?

Computerised Registers:

Schools should make monthly printouts (which should not then be altered) then bind them into permanent volumes and keep them for three years.

CHAPTER 3

PROMOTING ATTENDANCE

GENERAL

Summary

Identify issues	<ul><li>Analyse patterns of absence</li><li>Use consistent systems</li><li>Differentiate types of absence.</li></ul>
Assign appropriate responsibilities	<ul><li>Clarify positions and take the initiative</li></ul>
Take a proactive approach	<ul><li>Demonstrate commitment to promoting attendance</li><li>Use the curriculum</li><li>Liaise effectively with feeder schools.</li></ul>
Use rewards and sanctions	<ul><li>Involve pupils and local community</li><li>Define expectations</li></ul>
Encourage genuine "partnership" with parents	<ul><li>Develop "home-school contracts"</li><li>Define boundaries</li></ul>

If a parent who was thinking of sending a child to your school (or an OFSTED inspector) wanted to be assured that the teachers took the attendance of children seriously, where would they be able to see the evidence? Policies are important and management evaluation criteria have their place (this chapter contains models of both) but the real business of encouraging children to attend is done through personal relationships and imaginative use of the school's routines and physical environment. Pupils and their parents need to encounter the promotion of good attendance as part of their daily participation in the school. It cannot be left as an unspoken assumption until a problem occurs.

All schools benefit from open discussion about attendance and from drawing up clear policies which promote and encourage it. The purpose of this chapter is to help Heads to carry out an audit of what is happening in their school and to identify areas that require action. The primary focus at this point is on the resolvable and "normal" situations, not on those which are more complicated or which require much more substantial individual action (see *Chapter 4: Inter-agency Working*).

WHAT TO CONSIDER

Identify Issues

Analysing patterns of absence may reveal suprises, such as the amount of holiday leave taken during school time, differences between classes in the same year group or teachers using different systems of absence monitoring. Much authorised absence could be turned into attendance with different expectations. It is important to be aware of the range of reasons why pupils are absent from school and not to call all absence "truancy", for example (see *Chapter 4: Inter-agency Working*).

The primary day-to-day responsibility for promoting attendance clearly lies with teachers and all staff should follow appropriate procedures in the light of an assessment of the relevant issues. Governors should define overall objectives and strategies for meeting them in the school development plan. It may be useful to begin with an analysis of the previous year's registers. This might raise issues such as the following:

- Are proper policies and procedures in place?

- What is the major cause of *authorised* absence?

- What is the balance between authorised and unauthorised absence?

- Are lateness/family holidays/day trips a problem?

- Is internal truancy a problem?

- Are there patterns over the school year or differences in year groups?

- What do the children say about why they do not attend?

- Is the involvement of parents promoted effectively?

The above questions are appropriate for the governors or senior management team to address. Teaching staff should ensure that they are carrying out agreed procedures for keeping registers, identifying children with problems, seeking information from parents and so on. Too many individuals each making decisions as they think fit leads only to confusion.

Assign Appropriate Responsibilities

It should be clear who is responsible for what. Everyone, including staff, parents and children, tends to be more effective if they know what they are supposed to do. Do people have unrealistic expectations of each other? Is there a clear lead from the governing body and senior management team? It is preferable that staff take the initiative in raising the issue of attendance with pupils and parents. It is evidence of a "good" school if this responsibility is recognised, even if attendance levels are generally satisfactory. As with bullying or child protection, waiting until a problem arises is not usually adequate preparation for effective action.

A Proactive Approach

It is important to demonstrate commitment to promoting attendance at school. For example, when parents visit, are there displays in the entrance hall, interesting literature and defined targets? Is the issue raised at new parents evenings and are clear, written procedures given out?

Liaison with feeder schools should be optimised so that it is most effective. New parents and pupils need to see clear evidence that the school is committed to promoting attendance, through:

– statements in brochures

– wall displays and classroom work

– accurate information being provided for parents

– prompt action being taken, according to clear criteria, when a pupil's attendance is causing concern.

Although the DfEE's approach does not always make this clear, it is essential to keep the eye on *attendance* as the target, not merely keeping the level of unauthorised   absence as low as possible. Without this priority, everyone may settle for a lower level of attendance than could otherwise be achieved. The curriculum should also be used to raise discussion about attendance and to give pupils an opportunity to undertake their own research. This raises awareness and may also enable the school to act in a preventative way in response to identified issues.

Rewards and Sanctions

Issues to address include what the school does to encourage parents and children, especially those known to have a problem, perhaps in a previous school or where there have been problems with other children in the family. Pupils could be consulted over the type of rewards and incentives that might be helpful. Local industry, commerce and the community could become involved with school activities.

It is also important to strike a balance between rewards and sanctions. It is well-known that most children respond better to rewards than to the threat of sanctions. Parents do have a clear legal duty which they should be made aware of and defining expectations is helpful. But threats of court action and even prosecution itself will not improve the situation if the pupil or parents feel alienated and disaffected from the school or if there are major problems within the family which are seen as more pressing. Courts are only appropriate for a tiny minority of cases — there will nearly always be an alternative which is more likely to succeed in motivating the pupil or parents to improve.

Reward schemes for attendance, for example, should not involve only those who achieve 100% attendance but should also be careful to include those who show improvement, over a term or over the year. The reward has to be attractive, not what the school thinks the child would like. Public recognition, being awarded a certificate in assembly, for example, may be the exact opposite of what would encourage the shy, self-conscious child. Internal "report card" systems with lesson-by-lesson monitoring or accumulating stickers or merit points, etc may work with some children but not others.

Partnership with Parents

Partnership with parents should not merely be a catchphrase — there should be genuine efforts made to make it a reality, especially with the "difficult" parents (see later in this chapter). Heads might consider their own experiences as parents in other schools — what is it like to be an education consumer? What shortcomings have you encountered as parents or what good ideas could be imported?

"Home-school contracts" may be helpful in expressing a joint commitment to improving attendance but the danger of any element of compulsion is that they may be seen by some parents and children as setting them up to fail by making impossible demands which they cannot hope to meet. (They do not have the force of law and failure cannot be used as grounds for removing a child from the school.) Some parents interpret them only as an attempt to gain evidence against them rather than offering a genuine hope of progress through negotiation and compromise.

Schools are free to be flexible, albeit within certain limits. Pupils and parents need boundaries and to be clear about what the consequences of actions will be. Most will feel more positive about school if they can see that the school is sensitive to the needs of the individual — many will become more hostile if they are simply expected to fit in with expectations which may be quite reasonable for 90% of the pupils but which are not realistic in their particular circumstances.

Partnership should not be abandoned as soon as there are problems. If a school is serious about partnership and is not merely using it as a slogan to be applied to the "good" parents only, partnership will have to operate in more difficult circumstances, such as where parents have mental health needs, poor educational achievement themselves, different religious or cultural expectations, etc. Partnership will have to be carried out differently if a parent cannot read English, is a drug user or where the child has behavioural difficulties.

Partnership in promoting attendance often breaks down because there was not equal commitment — the school, parents or pupils may feel coerced. It may never be truly equal but, for example, bad news should never be given only by formal letters in brown envelopes, parents should not be blamed for what they cannot change and schools must accept that they could be part of the problem as well as part of the solution.

No school (unless it selects all of its intake and acts ruthlessly when there are problems) can hope to achieve 100% of possible attendances but many could achieve significant improvements. All staff should be conscious of what has been agreed as the school's written strategy. Promoting attendance is not about figures in DfEE returns or "league-table" positions — it is about children and their entitlement to education. Identifying that as the priority and planning realistic means of ensuring it are both essential if progress is to be made.

Evaluation Criteria — School Attendance

The school is actively involved in promoting and improving attendance through the implementation of a policy which aims to achieve agreed annual targets.

- Registers are kept in accordance with legal requirements and clear criteria are in evidence by which absences are authorised or unauthorised.
- The attendance policy aims to promote positive relationships with parents and the community.
- The policy is regularly monitored and evaluated and targets reviewed to bring it into line, at a minimum, with OFSTED requirements.
- There is close liaison within a pyramid of schools regarding transfer of data about pupils.
- A clear referral system is in operation within the school in order to maximise links between home and school and other agencies. The role of the EWO, crucial in ensuring good attendance, is clearly understood by all staff.
- Initiatives will be in place to promote and acknowledge good and improved attendance and to celebrate success in attendance and punctuality.
- Students are counselled about their attendance and set realistic, achievable targets.
- Continuity of teaching is encouraged in order to build the child's sense of security.
- Punctuality throughout the day will be monitored and prompt action taken to address problems.
- The attendance policy will lay down clear guidelines to monitor and address internal truancy.
- The rationale behind good attendance will be positively promoted throughout the school.

Source: "Developing Schools", Staffordshire LEA, Quality Learning Services (1996).

WORKING WITH RELUCTANT PARENTS

The ideal world of the DfEE's "parents' charter", in which everyone works happily together to promote children's best interests, may not always match the reality. Parents may have all kinds of "rights" but some choose not to exercise them, some do not know how to do so and some interpret such language as entitling them to behave as they wish. Schools have all kinds of "duties" but some operate by informal assumptions and explicit self-defences which effectively exclude large numbers of parents from participation. Such experiences lead only to frustration all round and to schools and parents viewing each other with ever-increasing suspicion.

Parents who had bad experiences when they were at school may assume that the same attitudes apply equally to their own child's teachers. There will certainly be issues of class, race and gender which create barriers in the eyes of many parents. Some may feel reluctance or aggression at the very suggestion that they visit the school, come to a meeting or speak to a teacher. It is also possible that, in an age of competition between schools, certain families may be seen as detrimental to the school's image and there could be little incentive to try and meet their needs.

There are several contexts in which such misunderstandings occur and these are discussed in the following text.

Attendance

Of course not all children attend school regularly. Some never do anything regularly — their lives are full of disorder and chaos. Their family may not plan ahead, or be able to anticipate problems. They may be juggling incompatible expectations, of which going to school is only one. In some homes, it may be only the children who are expected to get up and out by a given time in the morning (a quarter of households are dependent on benefits, for example). Going to school most of the time, or only a little bit late, may represent a considerable achievement.

Any approach to situations like these will require sensitivity, understanding and, above all, flexibility. Giving the family a choice between all
or nothing simply creates conflict. If parents are to be helped to see that
education is important, they will need to be offered solutions to the other
problems which are getting in the way. Threats just add more problems.
Try asking yourself questions such as "Why should these parents feel
positive about school?", "What is the child missing?", "What are we
offering?", "What stops them responding?". It may be that 75% of what
the school wants is acceptable at the moment, together with other strategies to move things along in the longer term.

Letters Home

It should not be forgotten that some parents cannot read, or not at the
level at which many letters are pitched. Some may ignore any letters that
look official. There may be too many circulars — how are parents supposed to know which ones are important? Does the school recognise the
need for minority languages? Some letters are unclear in what they want
the parent to do, or present them with ultimata or cold criticism.

Try imagining what it might be like for some parents to receive a letter:

- asking them to come to school to discuss their child's exclusion/be-
  haviour/poor attendance

- asking for money or giving details of the school's skiing trip (when
  they might be receiving Income Support or other benefit)

- informing them that their child has been removed from the school roll.

If it can be avoided, nothing important should ever be conveyed by
standard letter. Can what you want to say be said in person and *then*
written down in way which the parent understands and which takes
account of their views as well? Can the communication be both ways,
rather than being seen as simply requiring the parent to respond to what
the school has initiated? If parents do not respond to letters, it is important
to find out why — it is possible that there may be something wrong with
the letters that are sent.

Parents' Evenings

Parents have a right to meet with their children's teachers. However, some dread the idea. This may because they do not want to hear bad news (especially in front of other parents), because they think they will be "told off" as they were by their own teachers, or because school is an intimidating, alienating or unfamiliar place.

Parents' evenings often offer little privacy or confidentiality, no clear purpose to why parents and teachers are meeting and a great deal of waiting or frequent repetition. It is preferable for parents to see fewer staff for a longer period than to spend an evening waiting and having a series of short appointments with every subject teacher.

The school may wish to consider providing refreshments, displays, musical entertainments and so on, to make the evening more enjoyable. In addition, schools could try to arrange parents' evenings at a time when parents can best attend — early evening, for example, can be a very inconvenient time for parents with small children. Later in the evening might be better or it might be possible to arrange a creche. It may be worthwhile offering alternative times to meet. A few parents might need the teacher to go to them instead — this could be time well spent if it is important that a meeting takes place.

"Absent" Parents

Increasing numbers of children do not live with all those who are entitled to be involved in their education. Some parents are strangers to the school, turn up unexpectedly or are the focus of conflict with a former partner or the child. Parents can feel very hurt when important decisions are made without them or when they have not been informed of the child's attendance record, for example.

Many parents who are considered to be uninterested may not be fully aware of any problems taking place at school. They might not have been invited to a meeting, sent a copy of the report or given a chance to take part in ballots for parents, etc. It is possible that they might not be interested, but schools should not always take the other parent's word that this is the case. Someone in every school should have a working knowledge of the **Children Act 1989** in order to ensure that those parents who are living apart from their children are treated appropriately. Some will need special opportunities to visit the school outside the normal times or to receive more than the usual information by post.

There are plenty of other potential flashpoints which will require careful handling, such as:

- differences in disciplinary and behavioural standards

- disputes about how the child has been treated at school (this can be made worse if the school does not have a proper complaints procedure)

- parents with a mental illness, learning difficulties or with alcohol and drug problems

- times when the school has to take a critical view and when the parent is clearly in the wrong.

However, much depends on the kind of climate created — whether parents feel that they are part of the school or not.

Strategies for Dealing with Parents

It may be worth considering the two practical strategies described below.

1. Try drawing up a local "parents' charter", which sets out what parents can expect from the school and what the school can reasonably expect from them in return. This should not only involve the "easy", co-operative parents — the school should also include the views of those who might be critical or who would just ignore it if you post it out cold. Involve the pupils, the local community, the voluntary groups. Keep it simple and review it regularly. Make sure that it is not all one way, stating only what the parents must do. Include a procedure, independent of the school, for sorting out disputes. Be open to suggestions, talk to people about the school and seek their views. Make

sure that the charter is "owned" by the teachers and governors and actually put into practice, changing parts as necessary if they are not effective. Ask the parents what stops them from getting involved with the school and listen to what they say.

2. Look at how the resources of the school can be used to help the parents, especially those whose own education was unsuccessful. Large institutions which appear to have huge budgets and well-paid professionals often ask the parents to help. This may make people living on a low income very angry. How can the school be used to help the whole community, not just with recreation but with education? What skills do the parents have which could be developed alongside their children's? How could the school enhance the literacy, numeracy and social skills of the neighbourhood, to everyone's advantage? Parents will feel much more involved if they are benefiting too, their children will be more positive and the culture will be one which encourages participation rather than putting obstacles in people's way.

The chart on the following page outlines model internal school procedures for dealing with absence.

Internal School Procedures for Dealing with Absence

- Class teacher picks up pupil's absence and records in register as initially unauthorised (unless a note has been received in advance, eg for holiday leave, medical appointments, etc).

- Parent encouraged to confirm reason by phone on first day — the message is then passed to the pupil's form teacher. Telephone contact made with parent on same day if no information received.

- Routine (friendly) telephone contact from school on third day to check the situation with the parent, if the child has not returned.

- Arrangements made for work to be sent home for any absence expected to be beyond a few days.

- Pupil brings note on return. A decision should be made whether to authorise the absence in the light of the explanation provided and school's policy. Other "welcoming" strategies put in place after long absences.

- Any uncertainties over authorisation referred to senior member of staff for a decision. Parent informed in writing if absences not authorised.

- Children with persistent absence (for any reason) raised for discussion within school's pastoral system.

- Parents invited for meetings, written arrangements for authorisation made as required.

- Involvement of other agencies as required.

- Child referred to LEA Welfare Service as required by local procedures.

SPECIAL PROJECTS

In recent years, the DfEE has significantly raised the profile of attendance and absence issues. There has been a specific category of the Standards Fund, formerly the GEST programme (Grants for Education, Support and Training), to encourage LEAs to bid for new projects in partnership with schools. There have been several research and evaluation programmes alongside various changes to the law, mostly placing clearer responsibilities onto schools. This has all led to an increased sense of the key role of schools in promoting "core values" and combating "social exclusion", by stressing the importance of education and regular attendance at school.

Local School Initiatives

These have been the major focus of the GEST projects, in partnership with staff from LEAs. Grants have enabled LEAs to appoint additional EWOs to provide greater support to individual schools, (such as running "Circle Time" groups with children with low self-esteem or those who have been identified as likely to find the transition to secondary school difficult). Grants have also financed special projects to develop reward and incentive schemes and enabled intensive work to be done either one-to-one or with younger children as a preventative measure. Many have linked truancy and disaffection by seeking to reduce the sense of alienation which some young people and their families feel from the education system.

All of these initiatives seek to emphasise the importance of the individual school being seen to act in response to its own problems. Most place the emphasis on working with children and parents through the school and developing more positive relationships with the local community. (The projects tend to be pretty much the same as one another as the criteria for funding laid down by the DfEE effectively determine what kinds of work will be financed. Some other kinds of projects, which may have a different focus, have not been so successful in gaining support.)

The advantage of this approach is that it focuses the attention of the school on what can realistically be achieved. It encourages careful research and assessment in order to decide on priorities so that the whole staff can demonstrate a clear commitment to the task. It has enabled LEAs to give much greater support than would be possible from core funding and to undertake preventative work which would not otherwise have been possible. The disadvantage is that there tends to be a lot of "reinventing the wheel" by each school or LEA; the "extra" money has sometimes only been in place of reductions elsewhere; and the projects tend to be limited in their objectives, without necessarily tackling any of the "big" issues which affect school attendance, well beyond the confines of the individual school.

Examples

Birmingham Attendance Project

The Attendance Project has developed a "School Wise" course in partnership with a local FE college. This offers parents the opportunity to explore how they can participate more effectively in their children's education and enables them to build up training credits. Birmingham also uses pre-school workers to develop initiatives such as "Leading to Reading", "Home Learning" and "Shopping to Read". Weekly parent workshops which enable parents to discuss common concerns are run by curriculum co-ordinators, especially for new parents. This has led to a major evaluation of parents' evenings and new opportunities for parents and governors to meet.

Staffordshire County/Stoke on Trent City Council

Staffordshire/Stoke pioneered an approach to dealing with children on the streets or in shopping centres when they should have been at school. This was based on a "partnership" approach involving the police, local shopkeepers, schools and the Education Welfare Service. Shops displayed posters and staff were trained to approach children in a non-agressive manner to ask "shouldn't you be at school?". In practice, this approach meets more children with their parents than "truants", and many of them were excluded or authorised to be absent through illness or other excuse.

Among other authorities, Staffordshire has also developed an attendance incentive scheme, initially with local professional football clubs and more recently with the television programme *Gladiators*. This involves younger children collecting stickers for full weekly attendance which lead to various rewards and certificates. Additional welfare staff have also been appointed to undertake intensive work in particular schools/year groups, some of whom have been funded through the Single Regeneration Budget scheme.

Leeds Attendance Project

Leeds has a well-established project which, among many other things, has undertaken detailed research into attendance and absence data in key city schools. Schools are encouraged to look upon data collection as a means of assessing where they are now and where they want to move to. Schools in similar socio-economic areas with similar intakes had very different levels of absence, depending on sometimes very local factors which specifically needed to be addressed, (eg children needed at home, difficulties with homework, school–community relationships, etc). Staff were seconded to meet each other and learn from each other's experience.

Summary

The school has a legal duty to publish its absence figures to parents and to promote attendance. Various initiatives may be taken from time to time as required. If a child is not in regular attendance, he or she is being deprived of the right to a full-time education. Equally, parents have a duty to make sure that their children attend. The school is committed to working with parents as the best way to ensure as high a level of attendance as possible.

Model School Attendance Policy

Principles

[Add your school's mission statement here].

- Parents of registered pupils have a legal duty under the **Education Act 1996** to make sure that children of compulsory school age attend school on a regular and full-time basis. Permitting unauthorised absence from school is an offence and parents may be reported to the Education Authority if problems cannot be resolved by agreement.

- Every half-day absence from school has to be classified by the school (not by the parents) as either *authorised* or *unauthorised*. This is why information about the cause of each absence is always required.

- *Authorised absences* are mornings or afternoons away from school for a good reason (ie illness or other unavoidable cause).

- *Unauthorised absences* are those which the school does not consider reasonable and for which no "leave" has been given. This includes keeping children off school unnecessarily, truancy, absences which have not been properly explained and children who arrive at school too late to receive a mark in the register.

- Any problems with regular attendance are best sorted out between the school, the parents and the child. If a child is reluctant to attend, it is never better to cover up their absence or to give in to pressure to excuse them from attending. This gives the impression that attendance does not matter and may make things worse.

- Parents are expected to contact school at an early stage and to work with the staff in resolving problems together. This is nearly always successful. If problems cannot be sorted out in this way, the school may refer the child to the EWO from the LEA. He or she will also try to resolve the difficulties by agreement but, if other ways of trying to improve the child's attendance have failed, these officers can use court proceedings to prosecute parents or to seek an Education Supervision Order on the child.

- Alternatively, parents or children may wish to contact the EWO themselves to ask for advice. They are independent of the school. Their telephone number is available from the school office or by contacting the LEA.

Model School Attendance Policy

Procedures

The school applies the following procedures in deciding how to deal with individual absences.

1. *Illness and other legitimate reasons.* If a child is unfit for school, parents should contact the school on the *first* day of absence. When the child returns, he or she must bring a *written* note, signed by a parent for *each* period of absence. Absences will not be authorised without this procedure. In exceptional circumstances, further evidence of a child's illness, such as a doctor's note, may be requested. Other reasons for absence must be discussed with the school each time; notes will not necessarily be accepted as providing valid reasons. It is *not* usually appropriate for the school to authorise absences for shopping, looking after other children, day trips, etc. Leave may, however, be granted in an emergency (eg bereavement) or for medical appointments which take place during school time.

2. *Holidays.* All holiday leave in term time is at the discretion of the Head. Provided the request is made *in advance* in writing, leave for up to 10 days per school year may be granted, provided the child's attendance record is otherwise satisfactory. Leave may be refused where children have already missed a lot of work or at crucial times of the year (eg during exams). Requests for leave beyond 10 days a year will only be granted in exceptional circumstances on a case-by-case basis.

3. *Lateness.* Children must attend on time to be given a mark for that session, unless the lateness is unavoidable. Parents are expected to ensure that children are present at registration. Late arrival after registration without good reason is counted as unauthorised absence.

DEALING WITH ATTENDANCE AND ABSENCE — QUESTIONS AND ANSWERS

Q.   **Why do children truant?**

A.   There are obviously many different reasons and it is always worthwhile for a school to carry out research (especially at key stages 3 and 4) into what is happening and why. Children may not be motivated to stay away for the reasons we assume. For example, some research has demonstrated that, when staying away from school, children tend to be at home, on their own or with parents, rather than roaming the streets getting into trouble with others. The reasons may lie more within the school — perhaps the avoidance of a particular lesson, such as PE, or a conflict with a particular teacher. Pupils should not immediately be stereotyped as "truants" without understanding their individual needs.

Q.   **Does the child have to leave the premises to truant?**

A.   Not necessarily. If the measure includes those children who are not where they are supposed to be at each point in the day, an extended trip to the toilet can become what is sometimes called "internal truancy". The word "truancy" tends to assume that the child came into school and then left again or that they are are missing school without their parent's knowledge. Other terms are better for absences initiated or condoned by parents (see *Chapter 4: Inter-agency Working*).

Q.   **How can the school raise awareness about the importance of attendance?**

A.   Think carefully about your target group: is it the pupils, parents or the local community? A poster competition, for example can reach all three. The children do classroom work on the issues and design the posters, parents can be involved as judges or encouraged to come to an event to launch them and the local community can be asked to display them in shops, community halls, etc. Some schools have organised visits from theatre companies or mounted displays which are organised by a different year group each month. A dull letter to parents which seems to criticise everyone else is probably the worst way of addressing the issue! A school must be prepared to accept that while local media coverage is helpful, it may be necessary to manage the news by releasing success stories and countering headlines such as "local school admits truancy problem".

Q. **Are truants "children at risk" or just naughty?**

A. Perhaps in general they are a mixture of the two, but the language of need may be better than automatically seeing them as "bad". Many children are testing the boundaries or using school as a natural way of showing their anger towards parents, or even towards themselves. Simply excusing what they do or saying that it does not matter is not helpful and some parents need to face up to this. Some research has shown that young people are as likely to be the victims of crime while they are out of school as they are to be its cause. Children on the streets are always vulnerable, even if they do not think that they are. There are obvious risks when parents think their child is at school but, in fact, he or she is not. Children who attend school irregularly are also children "in need"under the **Children Act 1989**. This should entitle them and their families to services from local agencies, including social services, in order to promote their health and development, including their intellectual and social development, both of which are seriously damaged by prolonged absence.

Q. **How can an "action plan" help?**

A. It is essential that the *whole school* identifies certain achievable objectives and then keeps them under review. It is difficult to make progress on several fronts at once. It might be, for example, that the focus for this year will be on a particular year group or in reducing the amount of time which children have away for family holidays. This would lead to focused campaigns involving just some of the pupils, a theme for the parents' evening, or the school newsletter. The action plan needs to detail what the objective is, how it will be achieved and how progress will be evaluated.

Q.   **Do truants have learning problems?**

A.   Almost always, though whether they are the result of missed education or the cause of it can be very complicated. It is obvious that a child who has missed substantial sections of their course cannot simply be expected to step back in again as if nothing has happened. But they may have begun to miss school because they do not understand what is expected of them or because of some unassessed need. The involvement of special needs co-ordinators and welfare assistants will be essential in cases like these. It may even be necessary to disapply the child from the requirements of the national curriculum (see the regulations under s.365 of the 1996 Act) or allow a phased build-up to full attendance where simply coming back full-time after a long absence is totally unrealistic.

Q.   **When can we use alternatives to school for disaffected pupils?**

A.   There is much greater flexibility in key stage 4 than there used to be, although unless the child has an identified special need, this can be more difficult. Flexibility is always more likely to bring about an improvement rather than insisting on a child being treated in the same way as everyone else when they are clearly different. This can cause difficulty if some pupils appear to be "getting away" with something which many other pupils might also like to do, such as extended work experience or a place in a more informal unit. However, it is essential to keep "education" as the goal, not necessarily "school". Alternative provision, including FE colleges, which are available to pupils from 14 onwards in many areas, will normally require the school to part with any remaining balance of the Age Weighted Pupil Unit on a voluntary basis. LEAs only have the power to deduct it where pupils have been permanently excluded. Children should all remain on a daily register while they continue to be the school's responsibility (see *Chapter 2: Effective Registration* for registration procedures).

Q.   **Is bullying a significant cause of pupils' truancy ?**

A.   It is certainly an explanation in some cases. Unfortunately, many children are reluctant to admit to anxiety about the school, including any fear of bullying, for fear of losing face. Equally, some parents immediately allege bullying and refuse to admit that their child may be staying away from school because of some problem within the family about which they too may be extremely embarassed and reluctant to disclose. The initial explanation is often not the full story. At least in the early stages, the whole process needs to be as "blame free" as possible, based on a careful asessment of what is happening for each individual child.

Q.   **Is contacting parents legally required when children are absent?**

A.   No, but it is good practice if the school wants to do something other than wait for the pupil to come back and then sort it out. Many schools have a system of "three day letters" which automatically go home if a pupil has been away for three days without any contact from parents. It is possible that the parents do not know that the pupil has not attended and will reasonably expect the school to inform them at the first available opportunity. Other schools, with the support of additional funding, have set up a system of contacting parents by telephone on the first day. Obviously, these contacts should be friendly and understanding, not accusatory. Much depends on the expectations of the school's procedures but it is always better to create an atmosphere of vigilance and immediate response rather than giving the impression that nothing is likely to happen and that it will be easy to avoid detection.

Q. **One of our pupils has been away from school for some time. What should we do when she comes back?**

A. Getting this right is essential. Too many pupils tell stories of being made to feel self-conscious or, even worse, being deliberately embarassed on their return, for some of them at least not to be true. It is best to keep sending some work home, even for a pupil who everyone accepts should be at school and to keep up as many links as possible. Sarcasm and other forms of emotional abuse have no place, even when a child appears to have had no good reason for being away. The individual teacher may not know the whole story; inaccurate rumours can spread remarkably quickly in a school. A friendly and encouraging, if generally low-key, welcome is most likely to encourage the child to try coming again on the following day. The first day back can decide what will happen for weeks afterwards.

Q. **Can schools discourage a child from attending without realising it?**

A. The influence of parents and friends is obviously important but many children report that factors within school are more important than is sometimes recognised. Children who gave evidence to the forums on social exclusion organised by Unison and the National Association of Social Workers in Education in 1997–98, identified boring lessons and unsupportive teachers as key factors. If, for example, there is peer pressure not to attend or some other more tempting possibility, a child's attendance needs to be reinforced as a considerable achievement. It is sometimes too easy to focus only on the negative. There is nothing more likely to alienate a child than a feeling that it does not make much difference to anyone else whether or not they attend or do the work and that they never get any praise even when they do things right. Many parents give this impression — it becomes highly damaging if teachers do it too.

Q. **Is it right to reward a pupil for doing what they are supposed to do anyway?**

A. This can be a difficult issue, although it is always worth remembering that there is no legal obligation on children to attend, nor do they receive any reward for coming in the form of wages! There is no reason for them to attend, other than the fact that what is on offer at the school is seen by them to be of value. For the hard-working, motivated pupils, this may be sufficient, but pupils who feel they may not perform very well in examinations, may require something more. There has to be a balance between realism and appearing to act unjustly towards the children who are never any trouble and who come without thought of reward. Prizes for attendance, for example, can go to those who do extremely well and those who make substantial improvements. This makes it rather more fair.

CHAPTER 4

INTER-AGENCY WORKING

GENERAL

Understanding the Individual

All schools have some children who are absent without good cause. As outlined in *Chapter 3: Promoting Attendance*, a great deal can be done by staff, with sensitivity, good organisation and proactive intervention in working with pupils and parents, to ensure that promoting good attendance is at the heart of the school's ethos. This will be sufficient to deal both with the general issues and the vast majority of individual situations. However, once routine procedures and general pastoral care have failed to resolve the problems, there may be a need for the school to involve a range of professionals from outside the teaching staff in order to address the child's needs adequately.

These people or agencies may include:

- specialists from among the school's own team such as counsellors, special needs co-ordinators or home-school liaison workers

- educational psychologists, behaviour support teams and other LEA-based resources where learning issues are significant (the obligation to inform the LEA applies to all schools, including independent schools)

– health workers such as school nurses, the local Child and Family Consultation Service or child and adolescent mental health teams

– youth workers and others who work in the local community, including community police officers

– social workers from the social services department who are able to offer advice and asssistance to "children in need" (**Children Act 1989**) and their parents

– voluntary agencies, such as those working with drug and alcohol abuse or organisations which provide support to children and families, including, for example, young carers and children with specific medical conditions.

Much absence from school is not related to school itself but is a consequence of some issue in the child's wider life. Pastoral staff and others responsible for these areas should seek to develop local contacts with as many colleagues as possible in order to maximise communication and the effective resourcing of support. Teachers often say that they are not social workers and cannot be expected to spend their time sorting out social problems as well as teaching. This is true and it makes it all the more necessary that school staff build an effective network which enables them, with the support of the child's parents, to make efficient referrals to other key people who can assist in moving things forward.

This is especially important in relation to absence. It is dangerous to assume that a pupil is having difficulty attending simply for disciplinary/behavioural reasons (by the child or the parent). At its most extreme, for example, the pupil might be struggling with the consequences of sexual abuse and trying to call attention to this in the only way he or she can think of. In many more routine cases, involving an outside agency need not be seen as any criticism of the family, although many parents will probably feel guilty about their inability to cope unaided. Some children pose major problems and the last thing a school will want to do is to heap on a further sense of failure in either the parents or child if it is inappropriate.

Neither are truancy and poor attendance necessarily associated with youth crime in every case. This is a key concern of the Government at present. The majority of those who end up in youth offender institutions and even in prison do have poor educational experiences, as do many of those in the care of the local authority. Undoubtedly, failure at school, including exclusion and truancy, sets a young person onto a treadmill from which it is extremely difficult to escape. This is one reason why it is so important to tackle it at the time. However, this is not to say that a child who is not attending school will *necessarily* grow up to be a criminal or that their poor attendance is automatically a sign of rebellion and hostility to authority.

EWOs from the LEA should also be able to help in these situations, allowing for local conditions of service, even where there is no question of any need for statutory proceedings. They will not want to be seen only as the "heavies" who are brought in at the last moment to read the riot act when a whole series of more supportive steps could have been taken first. The LEA *must* be told of any children who have been absent for two weeks without proper explanation and those whose attendance has been unsatisfactory for a period of time. This should not be left to chance and internal school procedures should include ways of identifying such children and ensuring that they are discussed with the relevant officer. This may result in them facilitating the involvement of some other agency or in an assessment which identifies the source of the problem and steps towards resolving it, perhaps involving just one visit to the child or family in the first instance.

EWOs are increasingly operating on a model which does not necessarily mean that they have to do the casework themselves — they are as much responsible for assessment as for direct service provision. Many local "service level agreements" spell out this role in more detail according to the nature of the arrangement between the LEA and the schools in its area. There may also be other specialist advice and information services available to which the EWO can refer the family.

If the issues are defined as within the general area of enforcement, the first step in tackling the issues is for the school to make clear to the parents that the absence is unauthorised. It must be clear that the *school* (not the parents or the child) defines the status of the absences. A procedure for tightening up the authorisation process will often, in itself, resolve the problem. Many parents and children respond well to clearer expectations. If the school has never explained the problem and has responded to unacceptable absence by continuing to authorise it, families will not see why there is a need to change their behaviour.

This is especially important in defining the school's attitude to lateness or when parents are regularly providing trivial explanations for absence. Meetings with parents, written arrangements to clarify authorisation procedures or independent verification that a child is unfit for school, may all enable clearer ground rules to be accepted. EWOs will be able to assist in making these arrangements but there must first be a willingness by the school to define the absence as unacceptable by not authorising it.

Understanding the Absence

The response to unauthorised absence depends to a large extent on the nature of the behaviour involved. There are a number of reasons why a child may be experiencing difficulty in attending regularly (beyond the minor incidents which are easily resolved) and the nature of the absence needs to be carefully analysed.

Truancy

This term is best applied to those children who are absent without the support or encouragement of their parents (see page 29). This may be for whole sessions or when children leave school after registering. Some definitions of truancy do not involve the child even leaving the premises, eg avoiding individual lessons. This is largely a disciplinary matter, not a question of law enforcement and is best sorted out with parents. Children do not break the law by such behaviour. Even if the police become involved, there is no offence of truancy for which action can be taken against them, neither is failing to attend school, in itself, grounds for care proceedings by the social services department. Much can be done by schools to tackle such issues with vigilance, flexibility and imagination. Many children respond to incentives and rewards for improvements.

Parent-condoned absence

If parents are condoning, colluding with or even initiating the absence, this should not be described as truancy. This *is* a legal matter and persistent failure to act responsibly by parents may be the subject of legal proceedings, provided the absence remains unauthorised. More absences are probably under the control of parents than those initiated by children — schools cannot hope to detect all the examples for which untruthful explanations have been provided but they must try. This is likely to be a key emphasis in coming years as the Government is keen to emphasise that parenthood is more about responsibilities than rights and making sure that their child is in school is fundamental to being a responsible parent. Reminding parents that they do have a legal duty will be an inevitable part of any response to unreasonable absences, even if it means threatening the usual sense that schools do not like to risk offending parents. There is no point blaming the child in situations like these.

School refusal

This is more persistent than truancy. Some children do not attend at all or attend only very occasionally. Such refusal is usually an indicator of some deeper problem in the child's personal or family life, including psychological or psychiatric problems, such as depression and anxieties as well as major emotional, behavioural or learning difficulties. These are the most difficult children to help. Sending work home can be a very helpful way of maintaining contact and reminding them that they are missed, at least for the first few weeks of an extended absence. For some, the support of an Education Supervision Order (ESO) under the **Children Act 1989** may be appropriate. Prosecution of their parents is rarely helpful. Special educational provision may be required or even alternatives to school such as home tuition, at least in the short term. It may be appropriate to authorise some of these absences on medical or other grounds, provided this does not lead to the child receiving no education at all.

THE ROLE OF THE EWO

Where unauthorised absence persists, despite the efforts of the school and others to work with parents to reduce it, formal referral to the Education Welfare/Education Social Work Service may be appropriate. All LEAs will recognise that helping schools to achieve high levels of attendance is a primary function of the Service. EWOs are available for advice throughout the whole process. The school's attendance policy should make it clear to parents that the EWO is available to assist them with any problems in ensuring that their children attend regularly but that they also carry powers of legal enforcement on behalf of the LEA.

All LEA services, like schools, are under financial pressure and few are able to resource the Education Welfare Service as they would wish. Most have developed a partnership arrangement with schools which defines the support which is available. As individual EWOs will have a considerable number of schools to cover, perhaps as many as 20–25, it is not always possible for them to check whether children with problems have been detected (although formal register checks may be carried out in addition). This must be primarily the school's responsibility.

The role of the EWO with regard to non-attendance is as follows.

1. To identify, in conjunction with school staff, cases of unauthorised absence which necessitate further action and to advise on appropriate responses.
2. To assess the circumstances, in conjunction with school staff, which have led to the breakdown of attendance, identifying causes and other significant factors which may assist in resolving the problems.
3. To plan appropriate action in conjunction with the child, the family, the school and any other necessary agency, in order to resolve the problems.

4. To implement such action plans to support the child and the family in overcoming the problems.

5. To evaluate, in partnership with the school, the outcome of such action plans.

6. To maintain a written record of the work undertaken.

7. To initiate court action, if appropriate, on behalf of the LEA.

Clear referral procedures should be in place to ensure that the EWO has all the necessary information on which to act. Except in an emergency, it is beneficial if the EWO's visits can be prepared for and timetabled in order to make best use of the time available. *Written* referrals should be followed up with further sharing of information wherever possible. It is best to avoid verbal messages which may be misunderstood. Standard referral forms should include:

– child's full name, date of birth, address, year group, age and ethnic group

– details of the family situation as known to the school, including, wherever possible, the whereabouts of all those with parental responsibility, who is living with the child and whether the family is aware of the referral

– statistical information relating to the child's record of attendance, including grounds on which any absences have been authorised or left unauthorised

– what the school has already done in order to attempt to resolve the problems, including meetings with parents, letters home, contact with other professionals, etc

– the member of staff responsible for the referral and when they are available for further consultation

– space for the EWO to report back on the action taken and issues identified for further action by school / LEA / other.

Voluntary Casework

In many situations, difficulties are resolved by home visits, casework, etc undertaken by the EWO in partnership with the school. Officers may also make use of groupwork or other interventions as required. EWOs generally adopt a problem-solving approach which attempts to identify the underlying causes of the absence and then to devise strategies to resolve them. Referral may be necessary to other professionals and agencies where this has not been explored already. Changes in educational provision may be recommended, especially for pupils reaching the end of their compulsory education.

The normal emphasis will be on enabling the parents and child to take action themselves or providing an element of authority and structure which requires the family to confront the absence and do something about it. In a real sense, LEA officers have a right to be forceful with parents in a way which school staff do not and they should not be afraid to confront and challenge where appropriate, even without the power of a court behind them. If there are issues that concern the school, such as bullying, special needs issues or study problems, EWOs may seek to offer independent advice to *both* the school and the family in considering any necessary responses. Flexibility, imagination and increased communication are often the most likely ways in which to bring about improvements.

Where problems persist, EWOs may make use of a *written agreement*. This will aim to set out the steps which will be taken by all parties, including the child, parents and the school, to resolve outstanding issues within a given timetable. Agreements are not always possible but should always be considered prior to any more formal procedures. Many children and parents find this a helpful way of concentrating their efforts towards specific goals and outcomes, provided they are kept under review and changes made as required. Rewarding children (and their parents) for progress is essential, not just the imposition of greater sanctions should the agreement prove unsuccessful.

LEGAL ENFORCEMENT

Summary

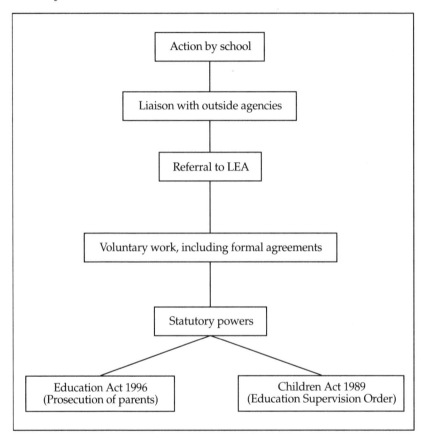

The LEA has a duty to seek to resolve problems on a voluntary basis if possible, so a procedure of this kind should always be followed first, including exploring whether a parent who does not live with the child can help the situation. Where this fails, written warning notices reminding parents of their legal responsibilities may be served. If use of the courts is being considered, the Education Welfare Service will call some kind of formal meeting under local LEA school attendance procedures.

Key school staff should regard attending these meetings as a priority and they have a vital contribution to make.

LEA officers always prefer to have the parents' active participation but some do not face up to issues until the last minute and encouragement to see the whole problem in a new, more serious light may still make no difference. Parents and children do not like being boxed into a corner and avoiding a negative spiral of blame and criticism will usually be the most likely way to succeed. If progress cannot be made by agreement, or if parents, for example, do not even turn up to meetings, consideration may be given to two avenues of action involving the courts. These are very different in their emphasis (see *Chapter 1: The Legal Framework* for more information on the statutory framework).

1. *The prosecution of parents* under the **Education Act 1996** for failure to ensure that their child is properly educated (s.444). This requires evidence of *unauthorised absence*, is heard in the Magistrates' Court and may involve the imposition of fines or other penalties. (These proceedings are only against parents, not the child.)

2. Application by the LEA for an *Education Supervision Order* under the **Children Act 1989** (s.36). This is heard in the Family Proceedings Court. The application is not punitive on either the parents or child and the LEA must demonstrate that an order is better for the child than no order. These proceedings are designed to provide children with a supervisor to "advise, assist and befriend" them and to give written "directions" to them and to their parents in order to ensure that the child is properly educated. The action plan for any such application will be fully discussed with the child's school in advance as school staff are key partners in carrying out the order. ESOs are still essentially focused on the parents in bringing them to accept their statutory responsibilties and do contain some enforcement powers but it is the welfare of the child which should be the driving force of any action (see also later in this chapter).

Statutory procedures are time-consuming and are not always effective. Wherever possible, other strategies are to be preferred. Prosecution is more likely to be effective as a threat than as a reality; some families simply do not worry about courts, fines, etc as others do, or it may make no difference to the behaviour of a rebellious or damaged child. ESOs may be particularly effective where the child's circumstances are unusual and the introduction of more structure into their situation may be beneficial. They are not suitable for children who are "beyond parental control" where the EWO is more likely to seek the involvement of the social services department, which has a wider responsibility in this context than the LEA. Educational alternatives may often be seen as a more realistic alternative to statutory powers.

Reporting to Governors

EWOs should welcome opportunities to contribute to the development of school attendance policies and to report to governors on the work which they have carried out in relation to pupils at the school. Much of the casework may be confidential but reports in the form of statistics and anonymous case studies may help to keep governors more informed of what is happening. Decisions could then follow about how the Education Welfare Service may be most appropriately used within the overall strategy of the school for promoting attendance and combating absence. Special incentive schemes may be available in addition to the regular casework. Training on attendance and registration practice may also be made available for governors, or as staff INSET.

EDUCATION SUPERVISION ORDERS

Ensuring that children attend school properly is largely a matter of persuasion, encouragement and negotiation. The use of legal powers is bound to be restricted to only a small minority of situations where parents have failed to exercise their statutory responsibilities and all reasonable attempts to resolve the problems on a voluntary basis have been tried and have failed. The most frequent statutory action by LEAs is to prosecute parents under s.444 of the **Education Act 1996** for the offence of failing to ensure that their child is properly educated, on the basis of evidence of unauthorised absence (provided by the school). The effectiveness of such action in actually returning children to school is generally very limited; parents do not always even attend court or pay the fines.

Children Act 1989

There is, however, an alternative power under s.36 of the **Children Act 1989**, which is used much less frequently or sometimes attempted much too late in a child's school career or after excessively long absence. Children can be allocated a supervisor to "advise, assist and befriend" them and to give "directions" as to how they should be educated. Such supervisors are normally EWOs or Education Social Workers and their role is to work with parents on a formal basis where they are not being "properly educated". As new powers to make Parenting Orders are being introduced under the **Crime and Disorder Act 1998**, it may be time to ask why this provision has been so rarely used and whether LEAs are failing to make use of all the resources at their disposal.

The power to apply to the Family Proceedings Court to have a child placed under the supervision of the LEA was seen at the time as largely a replacement for the previous power to use absence from school as grounds for care proceedings. This was, and remains, a misunderstanding which has tended to obscure the contribution which ESOs might make in the right circumstances.

A child who is refusing to attend school, despite the very best endeavours of his or her parents and professional workers, may, or may not, be "beyond parental control". If so — and if such a situation is leading to either "significant harm" or the risk of it — this is still grounds for care proceedings as before. The difference, and it is obviously important, is that *LEAs* cannot initiate such action as they used to be able to; only the social services can apply for care orders to obtain "parental responsibility" for the child and so change where they live, etc. Not attending school, on its own, is unlikely to give sufficient grounds; but this was the case before the Children Act as well. LEAs never sought care orders only because of absence — there was always a range of other risk factors involved. Care proceedings might still be appropriate for children experiencing multiple problems which are putting them at risk of harm, including failure to attend school with the consequent harm to their intellectual and social development.

The power left to LEAs is more limited and not for children in such extreme circumstances. But it is still significant. It is not a power to force a child into school (such a thing would never be possible without the child's co-operation); neither is it a punitive approach to either child or parents. It is, however, a positive opportunity to address the needs of children whose welfare is being threatened because they are missing out on education. The focus is the child's welfare; if that is being compromised, there is a *duty* to seek orders to address the issues. The welfare of the child is paramount in all work arising from the Children Act — "non-intervention" or working by agreement with parents are *not* more important than the needs of the child. This has been the same mistake as was made by those who put partnership with parents above protecting children in child abuse cases.

There is a widespread assumption that either ESOs are not needed (because we can achieve what is required by agreement) or, even if something is needed, ESOs cannot deliver. If a child's problems can be resolved without resource to the courts, this is, of course, preferable. However, there are many children who are not attending satisfactorily, who are not "beyond parental control" but where a more timetabled, structured and authoritative role for the LEA might be of benefit. There has been confusion over who this power is aimed at, not helped by limited Government guidance about criteria, and schools may wish to raise the issue locally in order to agree clear priority groups or individuals.

Focusing on Parents

ESOs are best used when *parents* are failing to deliver their educational responsibilities and the welfare of their child is being threatened as a consequence. Any Children Act order must be "better for the child than no order" but this should present no problem if the intention of the order is to ensure that the child is properly educated. It is always better for a child to be educated than not to be educated. The focus, as with prosecution, is still on the parents but on longer-term responses rather than a one-off court appearance, a small fine and no change in behaviour. It is a mistake to say that parents must be co-operative for an ESO to work — no Children Act order is appropriate unless there is some dispute. The guidance simply says that orders are unlikely to be effective if parents are *hostile* — there are many points between co-operation and hostility.

Parents may be indifferent, disorganised or inconsistent. They may be tacitly colluding with the child's absences rather than confronting them. They may be weak, powerless or lack basic parenting skills. They may have multiple difficulties of their own, including drug and alcohol problems, mental health needs, learning difficulties and physical health problems. There may be no grounds for leaving the absences unauthorised so no offence as such is committed but the child's welfare may still be threatened by missing large amounts of education, especially, for example, if the child has special needs. In all these situations, prosecution is certainly a waste of time or even impossible; establishing a formal relationship with the family through an ESO may well be much more productive. This emphasis on parents has often been overlooked but the focus is clearly still on parental failure, *not* on misbehaviour by the child.

Powers of the Supervisor

A supervisor does have considerable powers, although they will need significant inter-personal skills in exercising them. They can offer advice, etc and should clearly do so. They should be consulting closely with both child and parent about solving the problems but they can give written "directions" to the parent, for example about supporting the child at school, attending meetings, etc. Persistently failing to follow such directions is an offence. The supervisor can also give directions to the child, although this may be seen as less useful as the child cannot commit an offence by ignoring them. However, trying to use such a power unsuccessfully to protect the child, even from themselves, should result in a full assessment by the social services of whether other orders are required. This will not always happen but LEAs should at least try all the possibilities before giving up.

ESOs do leave the most damaged and unco-operative children untouched. They are not the solution to their needs and were not intended to be so, unless the child responds to the more structured, court-based intervention. Some do — it is not always easy to predict success and failure. No doubt many LEAs have failed to make use of ESOs on grounds that they lack the resources for what will be inevitably time-consuming and costly interventions. Schools will need to recognise that some children require a disproportionate amount of their EWO's time if they are to be helped. Greater commitment to ESOs may mean having to reduce involvement somewhere else, perhaps on those children whose problems are already insurmountable.

The active involvement of the child's school is essential if ESOs are to succeed. The supervisor must have the confidence of the Head and key staff and there has to be full consultation about any problems, including, for example, any possibility of exclusion or other major change in the child's circumstances. Supervisors effectively become another parent involved in the child's education and cannot hope to achieve success unless everyone is working together.

Conclusion

ESOs are not a magic wand, nor will they change the unchangeable, but a mythology seems to have grown up around them which needs to be challenged. Before we re-invent other ways of dealing with children's attendance problems, it might be as well to make better use of all the options which are currently available.

Main Findings of OFSTED Report on Education Welfare Services

• The effectiveness of the Education Welfare Service was heavily dependent on the quality of the support provided by the LEA.
• The range of work undertaken by the Education Welfare Service was wide and the workload varied considerably in scope and size between LEAs.
• Without exception, attendance was regarded as the priority issue by all Education Welfare Services.
• Firm leadership by an experienced Principal EWO encouraged consistency of practice and procedures and improved relationships with schools.
• The majority of EWOs were hard-working and committed to improving educational opportunities for children at risk of failure at school.
• Training opportunities for officers at all levels should be improved.
• Most schools valued the contribution of the EWOs with respect to attendance but were sometimes unaware of the full range of support EWOs could give.
• Schools did not always provide suitable working conditions to allow officers to be fully effective.
• Most Education Welfare Services were making determined and successful efforts to adapt to a changing educational environment and meet the challenges of the future.

Source: "The Challenge for Education Welfare", OFSTED, 17/95/NS.

EDUCATION WELFARE — QUESTIONS AND ANSWERS

Q. **What is the difference between education "welfare" and education "social work"?**

A. LEAs choose which title to use, although some LEAs employ only qualified social workers for this type of post. Very few of the social work training courses, however, recognise the particular role of education social work and the qualification may not always be seen as all that useful. In general, the word "welfare" is probably more appropriate as it identifies EWOs as concerned for the general welfare of children within the education system. This covers a whole variety of issues, not all of which are the natural province of social workers. EWOs certainly use social work skills, including assessment, family conferencing, drawing up agreements and devising problem-solving action plans; some are trained in counselling skills or groupwork. Some prefer not to be known as "social workers" because this title does not necessarily endear them to families with problems (or to Heads)!

Q. **How is education welfare funded?**

A. Education welfare, like other key LEA services such as educational psychology, is a "mandatory exception" from the Potential Schools Budget. Schools which are not maintained by the LEA have the necessary cost deducted from their budget centrally. This will fund a level of service determined by the LEA and is increasingly being delivered to schools on the basis of a service level agreement, which defines the services available. These may be at different levels for different kinds of schools. A few authorities have added in a financial element and delegated part of the welfare budget to schools for them to buy back certain services. Some schools "top up" their provision or employ additional staff themselves to carry out some of the non-statutory work. It is important to remember that the LEA is responsible for *all* the children in its area, including those in the private sector and those who are excluded or educated "otherwise", not just those children who are registered pupils at state schools. All funding systems also recognise the range of other welfare functions which the LEA has in addition to school attendance (see below).

Q.   **Is ensuring attendance the main job of an EWO?**

A.   Yes, but it is not the only one. LEAs are also responsible for playing an effective part in child protection procedures, administering free school meals and other benefits like clothing allowances, the regulation of children in part-time work and a range of other functions to promote the welfare of children, which may vary between different areas. Some EWOs are involved in organising school transport, working with children with special needs and those who are either excluded or at risk of exclusion. Many will offer specialist advice and information to schools and parents about "parental responsibility" and other key issues arising from the **Children Act 1989**, advise on bullying or drug abuse and help to resolve the frequent disputes which arise between parents and schools over issues like discipline, uniform, homework, etc. In general, EWOs do *not* like to be used for chasing up missing library books or school photograph money!

Q.   **How many EWOs are there?**

A.   Less than 3000 for a school population of over eight million children. This means that they are a very scarce resource, best used according to clear criteria.

Q.   **Is it best if the EWO is actually based in the school?**

A.   There are arguments both ways. Obviously with so few EWOs and so many schools, they can only be based in one of the many schools which they will cover. This can help in fostering a close relationship with school staff and being readily available when required. It also helps in building up a close relationship with other colleagues working to a "patch" system in the local community and with other feeder schools within the same pyramid. However, EWOs can feel very isolated within this setting as they are not teachers and may not be part of the school's professional support networks. Too close a relationship with teaching staff can be difficult as EWOs generally enjoy their independence and would not wish to be seen as simply another member of the school staff. They are, after all, accountable to and employed by the LEA, not the Head or governors.

Q.   **How often should our EWO come into school?**

A.   This will be a matter for the line manager to agree with the school according to local arrangements. Even the most demanding of schools could not expect to see their EWO every day, unless the EWO is physically based within the building. Simple arithmetic means that more than a few hours a week is probably unreasonable and, of course, the vast majority of the time which is spent working with the children and parents will not be time actually in school. Referral systems should now be based much more on the school initiating a written procedure rather than assuming that the EWO will have the time to call in and check the registers to make sure that children with problems have been identified. It is in everyone's interests to have the arrangements as clear as possible and to agree priorities and working arangements which are known to all staff and carefully monitored.

Q.   **Why do LEAs prosecute so few parents?**

A.   The procedure is time-consuming and complicated and will take up a considerable amount of the EWO's allocated time for a particular school. Not all staff and Heads feel that this is the best use of their time for what may be a relatively unproductive outcome. Schools must also be prepared to leave absences unauthorised in order to accumulate the necessary evidence and this is not always possible. There should be clear agreement in each area about the criteria for bringing a prosecution and what procedures need to be followed first. Decision-making should be according to set procedures so that suitable cases for prosecution are identified and action taken at the appropriate time. However, many situations of chronic poor attendance will not be resolved by action through the courts and resources are unlikely to allow more cases to proceed than have some realistic chance of being improved as a result.

Q. **Can Heads take legal action themselves?**

A. No, only the LEA has the necessary powers. Heads provide the evidence in the form of a copy of the register and, if necessary, a written or verbal statement. The procedures are becoming increasingly complicated and cases are sometimes presented by solicitors in some LEAs.

Q. **What happens when a parent is taken to court?**

A. They receive a summons which requires them to attend court at the specified time and gives full details in advance of all the evidence against them. The child is not required to attend, although some courts like to see them. If the parent does not turn up, some courts will deal with the case in their absence and they may impose a heavy fine, at least to begin with. Much depends on whether the parent pleads guilty. Most do as the offence is usually obvious; though if they have not taken legal advice, the hearing may be adjourned for them to do so. Defendants will not qualify for legal aid unless they are on specified benefits. The EWO and Head may be required to give evidence in person, although written statements are often sufficient. Some cases last for many months with repeated adjournments.

Q. **What penalties are imposed?**

A. If the parent is convicted, the court may impose a fine of up to a maximum of £1000, although they must take ability to pay into account and the fine may be as low as £50, or lesser penalties may be imposed, such as a conditional discharge. Many parents rely on mitigation after conviction to keep the penalty as low as possible, including the fact that they have done everything reasonable but the child will just not attend school when required. Some parents are prosecuted more than once as, if the child still does not return to school after the prosecution, there will then be an additional offence. The **Crime and Disorder Act 1998** is expected to introduce Parenting Orders as a new penalty which will require the parent to work with officials after the prosecution in ensuring the child actually attends. This will probably increase the number of cases being brought and may make prosecution much more productive.

Q. **Do schools have to produce their registers when asked to do so?**

A. Registers must be produced to authorised LEA officers and for the collection of evidence for courts. All schools should also make information available in response to any child protection enquiry. Registers must also be made available for inspection by OFSTED.

Q. **Are EWOs inspected?**

A. OFSTED carried out an inspection of a specimen selection of Welfare Services between 1992 and 1994. The report, *The Challenge for Education Welfare*, drew attention to the generally high standard of their work but also noted the importance of effective management structures and good working relationships with schools. Much depended on the commitment of the individual LEA, and, as there is no national standard, there is considerable variation in provision. A good service will have clear policy statements, defined aims and objectives and effective documentation. Many LEAs have been re-examining their Welfare Services in the light of this report. Now that LEAs are inspected on a formal basis, this will also bring all LEA services under closer scrutiny.

Q.   **Do EWOs have the right to go into people's houses?**

A.   No. They have no automatic right of entry under any circumstances. In general, most EWOs will prefer not to be in children's
houses without a parent present, though practice varies. With all
the concerns about the risks to both professionals and children
in the context of "professional abuse" most agencies are having
to rethink their procedures and to ensure that expectations about
what they are able to do are reasonable. Some EWOs will increasingly be trying to visit by appointment with parents rather than
simply knocking on the door when they are not expected, even
if this makes it more difficult to catch children at home alone.

Q.   **Can EWOs physically force a child to come to school?**

A.   No. Even under an ESO (or presumably under a Parenting
Order) they can only "advise, assist and befriend" and give
written "directions" to the child/parents. All other relationships
with both children and their parents are entirely voluntary.
Physical threats have no place in the work of an EWO and the
days have long gone when they could be expected to bring a child
to school by force. Even the police will have problems returning
a child to school who is violently resisting. This is totally unreasonable and counter-productive — the school could not itself
detain a child against his or her will, even once the child had been
brought in. Other skills, such as persuasion, patience and persist-
ence are required, as in all work with children.

CHAPTER 5

NARRATIVE CASE-STUDIES

JOEL

Referral

Joel is seven and lives with his family in a community of travellers. They have several resting places and, when he is at one of these, Joel is usually admitted to the local school for a few weeks at a time before moving on. It is now four months since he went to school anywhere and no-one is too sure whether he is still on the roll at his last school. Residents in the area where the community is now staying have been complaining about the children not going to school and a local councillor has written to the Chief Education Officer demanding that something be done about it.

Initial Response

Angela, the EWO for the area where the community is now staying, has a number of investigative tasks to carry out.

1. She visits the site in partnership with the field officers from the local Traveller Education Service. Other residents are ambiguous about whether he is there. They say he is usually there but is currently visiting his grandmother in the south of England. He may be back

next week. The EWO leaves a form for one of the parents to complete about whether they intend to educate Joel themselves with support from the Travellers' Tutor or whether they want to admit him to the local school, as they expect to be on the present site for the winter.

2. Attempts are made to contact the last school Joel attended, to find out whether he is still on the roll there. The school reports that they took him off the admission register after four weeks as neither they nor their EWO knew where the family had gone. The EWO asks for his (very limited) educational records to be sent to the LEA. The Head mentions that Joel has significant learning difficulties and is still at the pre-reading stage.

3. The EWO contacts the local county (community) primary school about admitting Joel (and three other children). The Head is reluctant, as a previous family staying on the site caused a number of problems in the locality and some parents have said they will move their children elsewhere if the school admits any more "gypsies". The EWO advises that the school, which is not full in the relevant year groups, will have to admit the children, including Joel, if that is what the parents request. The Head is especially concerned about Joel's learning difficulties as her special needs budget is already overspent.

Legal point

As Joel is no longer on a school register, he is not "absent" and his parents cannot be said to be committing any offence (unless it could be shown that they are failing "to secure his education"). However, his current educational status is unclear as he is neither a registered pupil nor being educated "otherwise". The EWO's first priority will be to resolve this issue. There is also the key question of Joel's special needs and the implications this may have for the provision he requires.

Initial Stages

No reply is received from Joel's parents about how they intend to educate him, so Angela visits the following week with the stage 1 letter for a potential School Attendance Order. There is some concern that the moment things become official, the family will simply move on again.

On arrival at the site, a boy whom she takes to be Joel runs off as she knocks on the caravan door. Joel's mother confirms that he is back and that she would like him to go to the local school. No formal letters are left and Angela arranges to take Joel and his mother to the school later in the week.

After a false start when Joel and his mother did not go to the school, a meeting is held on the Friday afternoon. It is obvious that neither Joel nor the Head is very keen on him coming to the school. Angela tries to build on Joel's mother's willingness to address his needs and especially the fact that he is significantly behind in his reading. Joel's mother agrees that this will be a considerable problem to him in future and, as she is a very limited reader herself, she does not want him to have the same problems.

Eventually it is agreed that Joel will be admitted from the following Monday, although he does not have the necessary uniform. Joel's mother seems pleased with the decision and promises to get his uniform sorted out over the weekend.

Legal point

The key issue now becomes the fact that Joel must become a "registered pupil". It has been agreed that the "otherwise" option is inappropriate. Joel must now turn up for at least one session so that he can be admitted to the admission register and for his legal status to be clarified.

Monday Morning

The Head rings Angela at 0930 to say that Joel has not turned up as expected. The EWO makes a visit to the site later in the day. Joel's father is at home alone. He says that he only came back from working away at the weekend and knows nothing about Joel going to school. His wife and Joel have gone away "for a few days". Angela again explains the need for Joel to receive education and his reading difficulty. His father does not seem to see this as such a big problem as his own ability to read is very limited but it has not stopped him earning a living.

The EWO still has the formal letter explaining the need for the family either to register Joel at a school or educate him "otherwise", so she changes the dates and leaves the letter. This means that Joel's parents must give an answer one way or the other within 10 days.

On arriving back to the office, Angela advises the Head of the situation and that she cannot admit Joel yet. The education records have arrived from the previous school. They confirm Joel's learning difficulties. There is also a confidential section about a child protection concern which was referred six months ago when Joel came to the school with extensive bruising to his buttocks. There is no indication of what the outcome was.

Angela contacts the social services and asks them to check with the previous authority whether the child protection issue was resolved and whether Joel was on the child protection register. Some concern is raised that Joel has not been seen since his father came home.

Legal point

Schools are entitled to keep confidential data about child protection issues which do not have to be disclosed to parents. As far as possible, this information should be passed in confidence to the designated teacher in the receiving school or the designated officer in the receiving LEA. Obviously this cannot be done if you do not know where the child has gone. In this case, keep the records permanently in case they are needed in the future.

The Following Week

Joel still does not arrive at the school and no reply is received from his parents. Angela makes yet another visit with the Traveller Education Service and this time Joel is at home with his mother, safe and well. Again she agrees to admit Joel to the school and Angela agrees to collect them both the following morning. This time all goes well and Joel is formally registered.

The social services have now traced the child protection records. The previous incident was confirmed as over-chastisement and Joel's father was cautioned by the police. Joel was not case-conferenced and the EWO/school are advised to report any further concerns immediately.

Problems

Angela receives regular calls from Joel's school over the next few weeks. His attendance is about 50% and most of the absences are not covered by a note. She confirms with the school that the absences have all been left unauthorised, although the Head is not very happy at the impact on her attendance figures. Joel has been admitted to the early stages of the assessment process for special needs and they are trying to address his problems but this is made much more difficult by his erratic attendance. There have been no child protection concerns raised.

Angela makes occasional visits to the family and it is agreed that a formal meeting will be held to review progress. Everyone attends except Joel's father. It is clear that his mother feels that she cannot make any decisions without her husband — it was only because he changed his mind that Joel went to school at all. She is worried that if the pressure is put on too much, his father will just withdraw him from school, make the family move on again and there might be more violence. She and Joel are clearly quite afraid of her husband. She is advised to seek help if needed and it is agreed to leave things as they are for the time being. The Head suggests that Joel's mother comes into the school a couple of times a week to help him (and herself) with reading.

Legal point

Joel is a "child in need" under the **Children Act 1989** *by virtue of his poor school attendance, his special needs and the past history of concern about his safety. This entitles him and his family to services and support but much depends on whether they are willing to ask for them. The threshold of "significant harm", or the risk of it, has to be met before anything could happen against their wishes.*

Crisis

A few weeks later, the school rings to say that Joel's father has been in and told them Joel will not be coming again. His attendance has been no better and, initially, Angela asks the school to keep him on roll while the situation is clarified. She visits the site and Joel is there with his mother. She says that his father has changed his mind and will not send Joel to school any more. Angela advises her that this might result in prosecution and that Joel needs to be in school. Some contact can be made by the Travellers' Tutor but only very occasionally and Joel's mother does not feel confident about managing the work in between visits.

After two weeks with no further attendance, the LEA calls a formal meeting under its absence procedures but no-one from Joel's family comes. There is some feeling that court action should now be taken to promote Joel's welfare. Angela thinks it unlikely that the family will stay around if there is any fear (however unfounded) that this could lead to Joel being taken away from them. It is clear they are still living on the site but could move on at any time.

Legal point

Joel must be left on roll and his absences left unauthorised if there is to be any evidence which could be used against his parents. Once he is no longer "absent" but not at any school, only a school attendance order is possible. This is far more complicated than prosecution. Parents must be resident in an LEA's area for proceedings to be initiated, irrespective of which authority the child's school is in.

Conclusion

In the end, the LEA agrees to begin prosecution procedures. Inevitably, as soon as the statutory letter is sent, the family are no longer there next time Angela visits. At this point, it is reasonable for the school to remove Joel from the admission register and everyone is now waiting for them to surface somewhere else. The prosecution fails by default and the case is closed. The school is asked to keep Joel's academic and child protection records for the time being.

ALLEN

Referral

Allen is aged 14 and lives with his mother and two younger sisters. He spends every other weekend with his father following his parents' divorce three years earlier. The whole family are irregular attenders at their schools, usually managing only about three days most weeks, although they are sometimes absent for longer. Mondays and Fridays are regularly missed. Allen's mother nearly always sends a note in with him when he returns. These say things like he had a cold or his mother needed him to help with the other children. The family is not on the telephone. Staff at the school often do not get an answer when letters are sent home and Allen's mother has missed two or three meetings arranged at the school to discuss his absences, all of which have so far been authorised by the school because of the notes. School staff are aware that Allen's father recently spent a month in prison for not paying a fine and his mother is receiving Income Support.

Initial Reponse

Colin, the school's EWO has known Allen's family for several years and colleagues even remember when his mother was a poor attender herself. She had Allen when she was only 15 and, in fact, her estranged partner, the father of the other two children is not Allen's actual father, to whom his mother was never married. Allen is not aware of this and has had no contact with his real father at all.

Legal point
*The definitions of the **Children Act 1989** can be very important in determining which "parents" schools/LEAs have to work with and their respective legal status. Although the man Allen calls "dad" does not actually have any legal*

relationship to him (although he has "parental responsibility" for Allen's half-sisters on exactly the same basis as Allen's mother), this will probably not be an issue unless she objects to his involvement. Should Allen and his "dad" ever live together, it might be wise to consider a "residence order" which would give him a legal status, especially if Allen's mother does not support the arrangement. The court could then decide what was best for Allen at the time.

Colin knows that there is little chance of bringing about a dramatic change in this family under current circumstances. He visits Allen's mother and tries to explain that the situation is serious. Allen should be in school full-time; he is in his options year when he will need to make important decisons about his future GCSE courses. Allen's mother consistently says that she sends him to school every time he is well enough but he has a lot of chest infections (the house is rather damp and cold in winter) and it takes him a long time to get over them. Colin arranges to collect her and bring her into school for a meeting with the year head.

Meeting at School

This meeting has a number of important issues to address.

1. Can more be done to stop Allen having so much absence through illness?
2. Is this the real reason?
3. Should the school continue authorising the absences just on the basis of a note from his mother?
4. Does she appreciate how much time he has had away from school?
5. Could Allen's "dad" have a more active role to play in improving the situation?
6. Is there anything in school which is making Allen reluctant to attend?
7. Is there anything outside school which is influencing him?

The school prepares a computer printout of Allen's attendance record in advance of the meeting and Colin (who is chairing the meeting rather than the year head to make Allen's mother feel more at ease) goes through it with her. Allen and his mother both admit they had not realised he was having so many days away and that he had missed so many Mondays and Fridays. A new explanation emerges at the meeting. Some of the absences seem to be because he cannot always get back from his father's on a Sunday and Allen has to wait for a friend of his to bring him home on a Monday morning. By then, he reckons it is not always worth going into school, especially as he "only has games" on Monday afternoon.

Legal point

The issue of children visiting parents in school time is becoming a common one, especially having "supervised contact" where there are complications such as a history of violence or abuse, or children visiting parents in prison. Where parents tell the truth about these arrangements (although some may not), they could be authorised as "exceptional circumstances" provided they do not happen too often. It may be necessary for the school to make representations to the parent, social worker or probation officer if the visits are disrupting the child's education beyond the occasional day. The kinds of problems presented in Allen's case would not normally justify absences being authorised, except in an unavoidable emergency.

Written Agreement

It is agreed with Allen and his mother that there must now be some kind of agreement drawn up about what they must do if he is genuinely unable to come to school. Allen will be taken to a doctor if he is not fit for school beyond one day and Colin is given written permission to check with the doctor whether he has been seen. The school will not authorise the absence beyond one day unless he has been taken to the doctor. Colin explains the consequences of leaving the absences unauthorised and that this could be evidence which can be used in a prosecution in future. No absences will be authorised just because Allen is late back from his father's — he must come in on Mondays, even if he is late.

Colin asks permission from Allen and his mother to contact his "father" and try to get him to take a greater interest in Allen's education. The year head, who did not previously have any details about him, agrees to write and invite him into school and to make sure he is invited to the next parent's evening. Allen's mother is sceptical but Allen seems rather pleased about this. As the meeting is ending, Allen says he does not have any games kit and the school agree to buy him some, provided he attends full-time for the next three weeks. The year head promises to explain to the games teacher that Allen will have to wear whatever he can find next week.

Legal point

Written agreements have no legal status and they cannot bind anyone absolutely but they can be helpful in defining objectives and setting timescales. They are not the same as "contracts", which may define the basis of the child's admission, although, at present, even these cannot then be used as the grounds for excluding a child from the school once admitted if the school judges that the contract has failed. Proper exclusion procedures are still needed. These agreements are more a written expression of partnership in which everyone makes promises, not just the child/parents.

The Next Six Weeks

It takes Colin a few days to get the agreement signed by everyone and circulated but things are quiet for the rest of the week. Colin writes to Allen's "father". Things go well on the first Monday; the games teacher provides the kit and Allen plays table tennis, which he did not know they were doing. He is absent on the Friday but comes in on the Monday with a note saying he "really did have a cold".

When his "father" gets in touch with Colin, it is obvious that he does not really want to get too involved. He has another family now and, although he did not mind looking after Allen when they were all together, he would now like to ease Allen away from his regular visits. After all the problems he has had with debts, he is thinking of moving further away with his new family to make a fresh start. Now that he knows about all the absences (the school had sent him a copy of the register), he thinks it is best if Allen does not come to stay any more weekends. Colin says he would like to come and talk this through as he thinks Allen will be very disappointed but his father puts the telephone down and there is no further contact from him.

The following Monday afternoon, Colin receives a telephone call from Allen's mother who has gone round to a neighbour's house in a panic. She says Allen has been "expelled"! Colin gets in touch with the school and establishes that Allen has been excluded for three days for swearing at a teacher. At the home visit, Allen explains that he got into trouble for not having the right PE kit. He was upset because his "dad" had told him that he is moving away and he will not be able to stay with him any more.

Colin helps Allen to write a letter to the teacher apologising for his swearing and promises to sort out the misunderstanding about the kit. But this incident, coupled with his dad's rejection, has unsettled Allen and his attendance begins to become very erratic. He starts going into town when his mother thinks he is at school, or refusing to get out of bed so that she has to leave him behind when she takes the little ones to school. She has found a job in the mornings and has moved onto Family Credit but this means she does not have the time to spend at home trying to persuade Allen to go to school. Once or twice Colin calls round when Allen's mother is out and finds him at home with other boys from his year group. His unauthorised absences are now over 70%. A meeting is held to review the agreement which has clearly failed but Allen does not attend.

Legal point

*Although Allen's attendance has deteriorated, it is difficult to see what legal powers would be useful. "Truancy" is not a crime and Allen himself is making all the decisions now, not his mother. He is angry, disappointed and disaffected. Prosecuting his mother will not change that — it might even reinforce it by appearing to place all the blame onto her, which would be very unfair when she is trying to improve her situation by getting a job. Allen's behaviour is not putting him at enough risk to warrant intervention under the **Children Act 1989** — he has just lost all faith in school.*

Conclusion

Allen still has two years of compulsory education left. He has missed crucial information about his GCSE options and there is a real danger of him dropping out of school altogether. Once he gets into Year 10, with a set of courses which he played only a nominal part in choosing, Colin suggests a fresh start. The local FE college is running a new link course which involves three days at school, one day in college and one day's work experience. Allen can drop some of his GCSE courses, concentrate on the basics and get some vocational qualifications alongside. The school will release him for the two days on the condition that he attends properly on the other three. It is his best chance, but will it work?

Legal point

There is more flexibility than there used to be but progress always depends on the child's co-operation. Education does not have to be in a school — work experience is now available throughout the whole of key stage 4. The school will need to take overall responsibility for such arrangements and can mark the register as "approved educational activity", provided the child attends a full-time programme. They will need to release at least a percentage of the AWPU in order to finance any alternative. Work-based programmes will need careful monitoring to make sure the child does not interpret them as being allowed to get a job, which is not legal.

FREYDA

Referral

Freyda, aged 10, has Downs Syndrome and is a pupil with a statement of special educational needs at a special school for children with moderate learning difficulties. She is supposed to come to school by minibus but is often not at the stop. Her mother sometimes rings to say that she over-slept, sometimes she is away for a few days without explanation. Freyda also has a considerable amount of time off through sickness and there is some concern that her parents do not always seem to think it is worth taking her to the doctor. Freyda also needs speech therapy but is often not at school to receive it or does not turn up for clinic appointments. The school has had difficulty contacting her parents but they always seem well-meaning. Other professionals who have been involved with the family feel that her parents probably have learning difficulties themselves and do not really understand Freyda's needs.

Initial Response

Mary, the EWO for the area in which Freyda lives does not know the family as she has always attended special schools and there are no other children in the family. The school has its own welfare assistant but as Freyda lives five miles away it is difficult to maintain regular contact. Mary talks the case over with her before making a home visit in the evening when both her parents and Freyda are at home.

The house is in a poor state and not very clean. Freyda is watching television and eating chips from the shop. She is reluctant to talk to Mary. Even this early in the evening, her father seems to have been drinking and her mother is very quiet. They say that they cannot really see what all the fuss is about — Freyda goes to school as often as possible but they do not feel there is much point as she is "never going to learn anything". It turns out that her father had an older sister with Downs Syndrome who is "in a home" and they expect the same to happen to Freyda in the long run.

Mary tries to explain that times have changed and that there is no reason why Freyda cannot benefit from education and learn the skills she needs to live more independently when she grows up. Her parents promise to try and make sure she goes more regularly. Mary offers to take them and Freyda to the next speech therapy appointment herself and encourages them to make contact with a local support group for parents whose children have a learning disability.

Legal point

Children with identified special educational needs can raise particular issues about the legal requirements for attendance. Their parents must ensure that they are educated in accordance with their "age, ability and aptitude and any special educational needs they may have". This is not just about sending them to school as there will be a variety of wider issues to be addressed if the child is to benefit from the education provided. In a sense, parents of such children have a greater obligation than others and more than just attendance may be relevant in determining whether they have fulfilled it.

Assessment of Freyda's Needs

It is clear that there are a variety of wider issues beyond simply seeing this as an attendance problem. Mary suggests bringing forward Freyda's annual statement review and a meeting is arranged at school involving the key professionals. Mary brings Freyda's mother to the meeting but her father is at work. At the meeting it is agreed to renew the attempts at speech therapy and to provide Freyda's parents with a new assessment of her skills and capabilities. She is doing well in school but there are signs that it is only in school that she shows any of these skills — at home she just sits in front of the television and is much less communicative. Freyda's mother is encouraged to join the local parents' support group and to let Freyda go to the "Gateway" club for children and young people.

Freyda's mother says that she sometimes has to smack her because she is "very stubborn and will not do as she is told". The staff try to help her to see that this may be because she is frustrated and bored and that greater stimulation and activity in her life will help her. They suggest a programme which involves activities sent home by the school and something each weekend to get her out of the house and meeting other people. Freyda's mother seems to have little idea of what her interests are and what she may be capable of doing with a bit of encouragement. Mary agrees to keep in regular contact for a while and to bring Freyda's parents to the school once every half term to see her work and meet her teachers.

Child Protection Referral

A few Mondays later, Mary is notified of a child protection referral over the weekend. The police were called to Freyda's house late on Saturday night. Her father had been drinking and had got into a violent fight with her mother. When they got there, Freyda was outside in the street crying and being comforted by a neighbour. The neighbour alleged to the police that her father had been "interfering with her". Social services were immediately informed and when they visited it was agreed that Freyda be accommodated in a local residential unit for children with learning difficulties while the matter was investigated.

Legal point

The police should always check whether there are child protection issues behind an incident of domestic violence, as this is a frequent risk indicator. They have the power to remove a child into "police protection" if they are in immediate danger. Only the police can remove a child in this way without a court order — the social services cannot do this. It is often better if the alleged abuser can be encouraged to leave the home rather than the child, although, as in this case, the child's needs may be such that a residential admission may be in their best interests, at least for a short time. No statutory powers have been used — Freyda's parents are free to remove her at any time.

The child protection investigation is inconclusive. Freyda's dad denies all allegations and the evidence from the neighbour is very vague, based primarily on things Freyda has said to her. Under video interview, Freyda is frightened and confused and makes no obvious allegation herself. Her mother agrees to a medical examination but this too provides nothing of significance. There is some concern that Freyda's parents will simply leave her in the residential unit. Her father has said that he does not want her home again because of the allegations.

The case conference feels that Freyda should be on the child protection register if she goes home. As well as the allegation about sexual abuse, there is also the report from Mary that her mother smacks her when she will not do as she is told. There have also been some examples of injuries reported by staff at the school in the past, which Mary was not previously aware of. There is general concern about the standard of care and lack of awareness of Freyda's needs. While in the unit, her school attendance is 100% but it is a short-term facility and she cannot stay there. There is some suggestion by the health workers that a residential placement with education on the premises may be best for her but this would need joint funding.

In the end, Freyda's mother says she wants her home and Freyda is admitted to the child protection register. It is arranged that she spends one weekend a month and some school holidays at the unit. Her attendance is generally acceptable and there are no further concerns in the short term although things are still a bit rough and ready. Her father keeps a very low profile and there are suggestions that he is now living somewhere else much of the time. The school provides a member of the "core group" which monitors Freyda on a daily basis.

Legal point

*Having a child on the child protection register places schools under an obligation to make sure that the child is safe on a daily basis. There need to be special procedures in place for making sure that on the first day of any absence, information is passed to the child's keyworker in the social services department. The general thrust of the **Children Act 1989** is that children should be looked after by their own families as far as possible, although not if this threatens their welfare. This can be a higher risk strategy rather than removing children but the threshold for deciding that parents are not fit to look after their own children is rightly high.*

Longer-term Issues

After six months, Freyda is removed from the child protection register as there have been no further incidents or concerns raised. Inevitably many of the agencies pull out at this point, the short-stay places are reduced and Freyda's school attendance begins to deteriorate again. Her mother is now on her own with Freyda and, although she sometimes manages to do things with her, Freyda still spends far too much time on her own watching television.

Mary is very concerned about Freyda and a formal process of consultation with the social services is held. They still feel that there are insufficient grounds for statutory action and that poor attendance at school is now the major presenting problem. After trying to convince Freyda's mother that she must get her to school more regularly, it is decided to seek an ESO under the **Children Act 1989** to try and introduce a greater degree of structure and authority into the situation.

Legal point

LEAs must consult the social services before seeking an ESO in order to be sure that some other action, outside the power of the LEA, is not more appropriate. The court must be satisfied that the child not being "properly educated" and that the order is "better for the child than no order", having regard to the child's needs, especially their education. They apply the "welfare checklist" before making any order. It is not simply an automatic process. Once the order is made, the parent is committing an offence if they do not follow the supervisor's "directions" and, should the child not co-operate, social services must make a full assessment of their situation if asked to do so by the LEA.

Education Supervision Order

The court agrees that the application is in Freyda's best interests and makes an order lasting one year. The action plan sets out what everyone will to do to address Freyda's educational, health and social care needs. Mary is allocated as the supervisor, with support from a colleague and welfare staff at the school who form a kind of "core group" to review progress on a regular basis. Freyda's mother co-operates fully and even begins to enjoy the attention. She starts to see Mary as a friend and, at times, Mary is worried that she is becoming too dependant on her. Freyda's school attendance is now excellent and, bearing in mind the deterioration once the agencies pulled out before and Freyda's long-term special needs, it is agreed to apply to have the order extended for another two years. Mary also involves the local parents network and makes a direction under the order that Freyda must attend the local "Gateway" club (as long as she wants to go).

Mary is aware that she cannot go on giving this amount of support for the rest of Freyda's education, which should continue at least until she is 19. It may well be best for some kind of residential placement to be identified, especially post-16. This is a key question to be considered at the review of Freyda's statement when she is 14 — whether it can be done will depend on whether her priority is high enough and sufficient resources are available.

INDEX

A

absence

  authorised 10, 15–16, 63, 99–100

    register records 21–2, 26–33, 40, 46, 59, 77

  four week period 19

  parental notes 26, 28, 31, 40–1, 59, 64, 99–101

  pattern analysis 47–9

  publishing of figures 15–16, 62

  returning pupils 59, 69

  sending work home 59, 69, 75

  special circumstances 32–3

  three day letters 68

  unauthorised 8–10, 15–16, 63, 74, 76, 80–2, 89, 97–103

    register records 21–2, 25–8, 33, 46, 59, 77

  unavoidable cause 10, 19, 28–32, 63

  written agreements 59, 74, 78–9, 87, 101–3

action plans 66–7, 77, 80

admission registers 9, 15, 17–20, 46, 94–6

annual printouts 17

  deletions 18, 44, 46, 55, 94, 98

  dual registration 20

  inspection 20, 46, 91

adults with parental responsibilities 8, 77

afternoon registration 15, 20–3, 34

Age Weighted Pupil Unit 68

alcohol problems 2, 57, 72, 84

amateur productions 43

approved educational activity 15, 21–3, 26–7, 104

assessment centres 20

attendance

  criteria 32, 34, 46, 50, 53, 89–90

  definition 5–6

  effective registration 25–46

  levels 2, 55

  monitoring 28, 53

  parent-school meetings 54–5, 59, 74, 80, 84, 100–2, 106

  procedure consistency vii, 3, 33–6, 46–9, 53, 59, 64

  promotion vii, 47–70, 71

  pupil awareness 65–6

  referrals 46, 53, 63, 72, 77–9, 89

E

D